Track Tests
Sports Cars

Track Tests
Sports Cars

Michael Bowler

Thoroughbred &
Classic Cars

HAMLYN
London · New York · Sydney · Toronto

Published by The Hamlyn Publishing Group Limited
London · New York · Sydney · Toronto
Astronaut House, Feltham, Middlesex, England
© Copyright The Hamlyn Publishing Group Limited 1981

ISBN 0 600 32205 X

Filmset by Photocomp Ltd., Birmingham, England
Printed and bound in Spain
by Graficromo, S. A. - Córdoba

Most of the illustrations in this book are from the archives
of *Thoroughbred & Classic Cars*; for additional photographs the
publishers are grateful to *Autocar*, Geoffrey Goddard, David
Hodges' collection, *Motor* and Maurice Rowe.

Contents

Introduction

In writing this book I must first acknowledge the kindness of so many owners who have given me the chance to drive their cherished possessions on road and track; sitting apprehensively at the pits, stopwatch in hand, while someone else tries, in five or ten laps, to assess the car that they have grown to live with more gradually must be traumatic. Some have even let me race their cars. Without such understanding this book could never have happened, nor could *Thoroughbred and Classic Cars* have had so many beautiful centre spread pictures.

In just over a decade I have track-tested nearly 80 different cars, first on *Motor* when some were modern cars, and have raced a baker's dozen in vintage and historic events; more circuit cars have been driven on the road. So the problem became what to include in this first track test appraisal.

I have always owned at least one old sports car and was brought up in the era when sports cars were still driven to the tracks to be raced, hopefully to be driven home again. Only latterly with the change from a 1955 Frazer Nash to a 1959 Lister-Jaguar have I joined the trailer brigade, the thrill of racing a 300 bhp sports-racing car finally outweighing the fun of using, and racing, a 140 bhp dual purpose sporting machine. It was the 1950s that saw this change in emphasis amongst sports cars that went racing, and the 1960s crystalised the difference, encouraged by the varying rules of the overall body—the Fédération International de l'Automobile (FIA).

It was logical, therefore, to start by looking back at the post-war sports and sports-racing cars, an era of great change, and an era which covers half my track tests; chapter headings have been reduced by a further half to select notable examples which illustrate the changing face of sports car competition. Not surprisingly, there is also a look back at Le Mans cars, as all but two of the 40 possibles had representation at the great 24-hour race. It is appropriate too, as the organising Automobile Club de l'Ouest has long been the tail that wagged the FIA dog in keeping sports-racing cars moving in a sensible direction. It is sad that the ultimate two-seaters have suffered in popularity over the past five years, and it is to be hoped that Le Mans will, once again, give the lead to sensible rules that encourage both large and small manufacturers as well as privateers to continue to take part. It is perhaps inevitable that the gradual departure from road-worthy cars has decreased the justification for the great manufacturers to take part, but success at Le Mans is still one of the world's great advertising attractions, even if all you can advertise is the company's engineering ability.

Before the Second World War when there was no overall championship, sports cars had to be production-derived even though special bodies began to appear in the late 1930s, the Bugatti tanks and then the streamlined 'GTs' from Lagonda, Adler, BMW.

The long war years gave engineers and designers

Oulton Park in April 1958—Stirling Moss in the 3·9-litre Aston Martin DBR2 about to pass Scott-Brown's Lister

time to reflect on events and cars past, but events of the immediate post-war years were based very much on a continuation of the status-quo. Inevitably therefore they looked at the situation as racing ended. In Grand Prix racing it was clear that no one would be able to afford the mighty extravagance of the Mercedes and Auto-Union teams, and that a post-war formula would follow the voiturettes; thus the new BRM was modelled on the Alfettas and the results of that Tripoli race when Mercedes produced their W165 in record time.

In the sports car world Le Mans had been one landmark of continuity but the Mille Miglia, more road car orientated, was as important in motoring design and development. The final pre-war race in Europe was the 1940 Mille Miglia, or Brescia GP, run over 9 laps of a triangular circuit near Brescia, 102¼ miles of very fast roads. It saw the 2½-litre Alfas and 3-litre Delages eclipsed by the 2-litre BMW 328s, and it saw the birth of Enzo Ferrari as a constructor with the 815—Ferrari then, as now, denoting models by a combination of cylinder number (8) and overall capacity (1·5-litres), reversing the policy of Alfa Romeo whom he had recently left.

What was significant about that race was the high average speeds over far from smooth roads; aerodynamics and suspension design became as important as engine power and light weight. Ferrari, Alfa and BMW had all made use of the Touring Superleggera construction with a basic twin-tube chassis reinforced by a multiplicity of small tubes over which the body was shaped and wrapped. The underside was clean too. But the winner was a closed coupe, the BMW that had won its class at Le Mans in 1939; that and another BMW had slight high speed stability problems on the long straights—aerodynamic development was still in its infancy, but its advantages were proven.

Suspension design showed little that was new; BMW merely continued with their proven wishbone plus transverse leaf front and live axle rear suspension that had set them apart as early as the

1934 Alpine Trial with the 315. Alfa used the trailing arm front suspension with swing axles at the rear which had characterised the early Auto-Unions—with less rear weight they weren't as frightening.

Thus war-time thoughts switched away from the slim-line body with cycle wings to the all-enveloping coachwork like the BMW—the Alfas and Ferrari retained a separate wing line although it was attached to the body. But, as ever, ideals couldn't be brought in overnight and cycle-winged sports cars derived from the 1930s were the major supporters of the early post-war sports car races, hence I have chosen the Lago-Talbot to open the book.

It wasn't until 1953 that the FIA introduced a sports-car championship. Until then the rules continued much as before the war—production-derived cars with the chassis, suspension and engine block about all that needed to be retained. Le Mans however allowed prototypes to be run and in 1952 they banned cycle wings.

Although that 1940 Mille Miglia may have sparked many subsequent designs, only one participant, Ferrari, reaped a personal benefit; Germany was forbidden to take part in FIA events until 1952, which ruled out BMW, Alfa Romeo eschewed sports car racing while Delage and Delahaye had merged to die together after the war, and only Talbot remained of pre-war front runners to fight again.

Some of what follows has appeared already in *Motor* or *Thoroughbred and Classic Cars* but it has been edited and updated in the light of later knowledge, while the place of the car in the overall racing scene has been added. Most of the photographs, though, will be different from those previously published.

I have enjoyed looking back over many track miles, not least because this has been the first chance to arrange everything chronologically, to demonstrate steady development and the effect that the rules have had on this.

Contrast in designs at the Nürburgring in 1964—the lone Ford GT40, an AC Cobra, the '64 Ferrari GTO of Parkes and Guichet which was placed second in the 1000 km, another Cobra and a Porsche 904

Lago-Talbot

Although I originally drove this car back in 1971 without its wings on, it is a dual purpose car, a classic French compromise of a Grand Prix car constructed as a 1½-seater to enable it to run in sports car events as well. Its owner, then and now, uses it as a Grand Prix car, sports-racing car and road car.

Inevitably back in 1949 and 1950 the sports car world was rather upset that a thinly disguised Grand Prix car could run amongst them, but that rather neglected the fact that the Lago was derived from a sports car in the first place.

Those single seater Lagos had the classic line of the real racing car that small boys used to draw — the long bonnet tapering down to a small cowl, the cockpit with the driver crammed up against the steering wheel with plenty of elbow room through the cutaway sides, and the long faired tail with the filler cap on top. They were known for their fantastic torque from the 4½-litre six and the way they pulled out of corners with a stream of tyre

smoke trailing from the inside wheel for 100 yards.

Having driven one in the wet at Silverstone I can vouch for the fantastic torque as well as the negligible grip from big but narrow 18 in racers. This one belonged to Richard Pilkington and is one of the 1½-seaters which could double as sports or GP cars; it thus doesn't have the sculpted fairing of the single seaters. About the only technical difference is that the single seater driveline is offset to the right via spur gears behind the gearbox, while the 1½-seater has its engine slightly out of line to give more seat space to the right-hand driver. The gearbox is a Wilson-type preselector with French markings for 'marche arriere' (MA) as reverse, 'point mort' (PM) as neutral and 1,2,3,4.

The seating position is typically old fashioned with the large steering wheel nicely placed for some powerful heaving—I'm told Duncan Hamilton drove trucks to tune up his forearms in preparation for racing his Lagos.

Richard Pilkington taking part in the 1978 Le Mans historic event

Talbot-Lago appears on the rocker boxes, despite popular use of the inverted form

Following pages: versatility—Pilkington using his Lago in Grand Prix form at the Nürburgring

Once I selected 2 for the push start—one of the single seaters has a neat comfortable jack plug arrangement at the back for instant starting with remote batteries—it fired quickly and because of its high gearing and fast tickover wanted to leap off across the paddock, which meant slipping the 'clutch' or the bands on the epicyclics. It was streaming with rain and I was wearing goggles. By the time I had emerged from the paddock exit and on to the pit ramp I couldn't see a thing. Off came the goggles and the rain really stung by the time I was halfway round the circuit paddling through Maggotts. I put the goggles back again, the steam cleared quickly—that lasted until we had negotiated Becketts and were halfway down the Club straight. Goggles down again, then back for Woodcote (sometimes), off again, then back for Copse. Two or three times a lap my wet face steamed the inside into opacity; mastering this situation left little time to do any constructive thinking about the car. The mirror afforded an excellent view of a cloud of spray so an occasional glance over the shoulder and a look across Becketts sufficed to keep me aware of any approaching vehicles—there were few other fools around.

I had been told that the hydraulic brakes were a bit spongy and needed pumping. I wasn't going so fast that the engine didn't suffice—select third and a quick heel and toe-blip, with the heel more effective than the toe. But the torque was impressive especially pottering through Becketts at about 1500 rpm in third giving tentative squeezes on the throttle pedal, the elbows poised to apply the appropriate opposite lock half a second later. The pull was absolutely even from 1500 rpm onwards with a change at around 4000 rpm, or 5000 if you are the brave owner/driver; brave in the wet that is. I eased the car up to about 3800 rpm in top which is likely to have been foolishly near 100 mph, but having got it twitching once or twice through sheer power even in third, I decided to leave full throttle impressions until a drier session.

The steering, which may well be heavy in the dry, was extremely light with the front wheels perched on a wall of water, which suggests that the box itself is free enough at least! It seemed low geared, but this may have been an impression from the awkwardness of getting the close-up steering wheel over to the other lock in a hurry. The open exhaust bayed in reproach, but it never fluffed despite rain and low revs. I learned nothing of its roadholding, although it is said to be quite good if you work for it, but at 2016 lb unladen it was the heaviest GP car of its time and with early pattern 6.00 × 18-in tyres there isn't a lot of rubber on the road to stop it sliding.

One more thing I learned was that hand signals have to be executed with care. With all that rain and spray I wanted to make my pit-turn signal prominent, so I wriggled into an upright position after sheltering behind the aeroscreen and raised an arm. I felt a sudden stinging pain in my elbow . . . I had caught it on the rear wheel. There's a lot you have to think about when you drive a real racer from the classic era.

The origins of this car are a little obscure. The single seaters had offset gearing at the back of the gearbox, whereas this one has an offset engine with a straight driveline with only a slight difference in half-shaft lengths. So presumably it was a 1½-seater of the type that Rosier used to win at Le Mans in 1950. A similar 1½-seater was used by Sommer in the French GP at Rheims in 1950. But this car was acquired by Georges Grignard and rebodied into a full two-seater by Moto in 1953; it was entered for Le Mans in 1954 but at Montlhéry in April Guy Mairesse overturned it during practice and was killed.

In 1958 Richard Pilkington went to Paris to get some Talbot road spares. By this time Tony Lago had sold all the competition remains to Grignard, and Richard went to have a look. The car now owned by Bob Roberts was for sale, but round the back was the ex-Mairesse car still in shunted condition. Richard went back in 1959, cobbled it together and drove it home. Once back the car was stripped and the chassis straightened by Rubery Owen, the two-seater body was knocked back into shape and the car used in Goodwood handicaps in the early 1960s. It also ran in the odd Pomeroy Trophy meeting after that, which was where I first saw it. Richard did one Historic Sports race at Castle Combe, but early in 1970 he started the task of restoring the car to its original 1½-seater condition. Everything was taken apart and a new body was styled from photographs by Peels of Kingston. It was completed the day before I drove it at Silverstone.

Apart from the transfer box and the axle casing with an offset final drive, the chassis is identical to that of the GP cars, a deep boxed girder frame tapering down and under the axle. It is cross-braced and the engine is four-point mounted to give some added stiffness. The rear suspension is just a pair of simple leaf springs passing under the axle to rear shackles with pivots below the springs. The prop shaft is very short, particularly on the single-seaters with the transfer box. At the front, large fabricated arms operate Houdaille vane-type shock absorbers in line with the pivot axis, and separate Hartford friction shock absorbers are mounted inboard. A transverse leaf spring clamped at its centre gives quite long if flexible lower links. Damping at the rear is provided by Hartfords and telescopics.

The engine design started life back in 1938 when Tony Lago used Becchia's 3-litre six coupled to a Paris version of the Wilson pre-selector gearbox in a Delahaye chassis. This was joined by a 4-litre which had a single side camshaft and short pushrods operating unequal length rockers on top of the head to allow hemispherical combustion chambers. After the war this was developed into the 4½-litre with twin high camshafts, Riley style. It has seven main bearings and the camshafts are gear driven.

The earlier post-war cars had six-plug heads, but from 1950 on 12-plug heads were available although still with a single magneto with a double-ended rotor arm. The lubrication system always characterised these Lagos; their oil cooler fins in the scuttle top are very effective. They aren't just

'Grand Prix sports car' —
Rosier at Le Mans in
1950 with the victorious
Talbot-Lago

radiation fins, but tubes through which the oil flows from one gallery to another. It is a dry sump system with one scavenge and one pressure pump.

The 1948-49 cars had Bendix operation of their vast aluminium finned brake drums which must be nearly 17 in in diameter inside the 18-in wheel; later cars had a twin circuit hydraulic system with twin leading shoe front brakes.

In design the Lagos followed on where the Delahayes left off before the war. They were never the last word in sophistication with a basic chassis and only about 250 bhp from their long stroke $4\frac{1}{2}$-litre engines, but they had plenty of useable torque and a maximum speed as fast as most at around 155 mph. Their heyday came in the years of the $4\frac{1}{2}$-litre unblown, $1\frac{1}{2}$-litre blown formula from 1947-51. Rosier was the star driver and notched up three GP wins, and Chiron won the French GP in 1947. Fastest of the opposing cars then were the supercharged $1\frac{1}{2}$-litre Alfa Romeo before the more efficient unblown cars, like the Ferrari, were introduced.

Tony Lago was the Italian born director of the

Sunbeam–Talbot–Darracq combine formed in 1919. The Talbot part came about with the acquisition of the English design rights of the French Clement by the Earl of Shrewsbury and Talbot, from 1903. From 1920 on, the French products were known as Talbot Darracqs. The finances of the combine were badly hit by devaluation of the Franc around 1923, but it was the failure of the English part over the 1929 slump that eventually led to the break-up. The Rootes group acquired Sunbeam and Talbot while M. Lago retained Talbot (silent T) and Darracq. In France the cars continued to be known as Talbots; the English liked to differentiate between their own Roesch designs and those of M. Lago, hence Lago-Talbot.

Richard Pilkington still races the car frequently in historic events and it is now going quicker than ever, mostly thanks to improves brakes. The engine too has been rebuilt but it survives very well without requiring major attention, one of the virtues of adapting a touring engine. The Lago was a Gallic compromise that enjoyed the best of both worlds.

13

Frazer Nash, and BMW

Few cars have been as consistently versatile as the Frazer Nash whatever the era. Before the Second World War they were as at home on trials, rallies and race tracks as they were fun on the open road. After the war, the new generation may have become a bit expensive for muddy trials but their other virtues remained; Eric Winterbottom's feat of finishing fourteenth at Le Mans in 1951 with a Le Mans Replica (named after the third place gained by Aldington and Culpan at Le Mans in 1949) and then driving on down to the Alpine Trial to record a class win and take a Coupe des Alpes is typical.

However the post-war Frazer Nash stemmed from the association that H. J. Aldington had formed with BMW after the German 315s had carried all before them in the 1934 Alpine. Aldington had taken over Archie Frazer–Nash's company in 1928 and had subsequently been joined by his brothers W.H. and D.A.

Versatile though the chain-gang 'Nashes were, it was not unreasonable to realise that they had limitations in ultimate performance for which

forgiving handling could not compensate for ever. Forming an association with a promising overseas company and acting as importers was a sound way to sustain the name and its reputation as a sporting marque, and the Frazer Nash–BMW was born. The association continued to the outbreak of war by which time the BMW 328 was the sporting flag-bearer and trend-setter.

After the war the brothers' association with BMW enabled them to make rapid contact with the remaining engineers and in the course of one visit they managed to bring home one of the open 1940 Mille Miglia cars in place of one of their own that had been crashed in Germany before the war and hadn't survived its incarceration.

This, with the support of BMW, was to become the basis of the post-war Frazer Nash, while H. J. Aldington negotiated for Bristol to become involved in car production with the touring equivalent, and to make the engine available to Frazer Nash to their own FNS specification. Accordingly it was arranged that pre-war designer Fritz Fiedler

Sleek lines of the 1940 Mille Miglia BMW, which strongly influenced post-war designers (the author at Prescott—hence the auxiliary strut on the grille)

should come over and work for H.J. at Bristol and Frazer Nash. Thus engine drawings and many other plans came over to England to establish Bristol and re-establish Frazer Nash, with metric dimensions converted to standard British measurements. The new Frazer Nash was announced in late 1946 as that 1940 Mille Miglia car converted to right-hand drive, like the pre-war Frazer Nash–BMWs, and adorned with a Frazer Nash grille. It was in that form that I acquired it in 1966. Frazer Nash had kept the car until 1949 by which time it had lent its shape and name to the Mille Miglia 'Nash amongst others; it was sold to Gillie Tyrer who raced it extensively for the next two years and took FIA class records at 132 mph and established it as the fastest production sports car over the standing kilometre, beating Sutton in the Works Jaguar XK120. It then went to Ernest McMillan who continued racing with it, using a Bristol BS4 power unit as well as using a detachable hard-top for GT racing. I bought it from Chris Horridge who had kept it in a barn for ten years, using it only very occasionally.

At that time I knew nothing particular about the 1940 Mille Miglia, but it rapidly became clear that it was one of the works cars, which had been acknowledged twenty years earlier, but forgotten in between. The BMW grille shape was still evident underneath rivets and filler, so I had it restored to that form.

It was the peak of the works development following on from the original 315 with its braced twin-tube chassis, wishbone and transverse leaf front suspension, and leaf-sprung live rear axle similar to the earlier car. Its engine was the famous 328 design that Rudolf Schleicher had developed from the ordinary pushrod 2-litre six. It was a masterpiece of expediency to create a hemi-head casting which could be mated to a normal block without going to the expense of overhead cam-shafts, or even increasing pushrod hole sizes to angle them and retain reasonably short rockers for valves on the opposite side. Thus the design used two

rocker shafts; inlet pushrods acted directly on rocker arms that pushed inlet valves outboard of them—the inlet ports were vertical in the centre, giving an extremely efficient downdraught tract; exhaust pushrods actuated bellcranks with further short transverse pushrods running in bonded-in tubes to operate rockers on the opposite side. Properly set up for clearances it rarely needed adjustment, proving capable of over 6000 rpm in its ultimate form. It sounds like someone shaking a tin can with knitting needles inside.

In its first production form the 328 was producing around 80 bhp at 4500 rpm; by the time the Mille Miglia came up four years later the 1971 cc 'six' was producing 130 bhp. Mine was redeveloped to roughly that output using sundry inter-changeable Bristol components for the longevity of superior metal.

Other differences over the standard 328 included a lower engine, leaf spring mountings that were nearly horizontal to reduce the roll oversteer, inherent in a standard 328, and a non-detachable slippery body mounted on small tubes.

As a road and track car it was superb, with the limiting factor on the circuits being brakes—too small and prone to overheating—and the inside rear wheel would lift when cornering hard almost before oversteer set in; this happens to a greater extent on standard 328s. The driving position wasn't brilliant, being too close to the steering wheel, but there wasn't much one could do about that as the cockpit length is short; however the steering itself was excellent, light, responsive and full of feel.

So although it was well ahead of its time the 328 had some shortcomings, of which BMW were doubtless aware, because the Nashes had a revised rear axle location, although they retained the same upper transverse leaf spring with lower wishbone and integral lever arm damper on the front. Like the 326 BMW the rear location used an upper A-bracket while the lower fore-and-aft location was via links on the ends of levers attached to the longitudinal torsion bars; fore and aft location depended on the rigidity of these links and their bushes. While this tied the axle down reasonably effectively it gave a very high roll centre; this is acceptable on a saloon to keep roll angles down despite soft springing, but is not really suited to a lightweight two-seater as it tends to unload the inside rear wheel.

I have driven two of the narrow little Le Mans Replicas. The first was the ex-Tony Crook Mk. I PPG 1 owned at that time by Frank Sytner. It displayed all the updated agility of the pre-war Nashes, light, bouncy, precise in response with a cockpit width that heightens the vintage feel with elbows out in the rain. The Bristol-built gearbox is much stronger than that of the 328s but the whippy wand lever is not at all suited to a sporting car, although the narrow cockpit would have made a remote lever difficult.

The next Le Mans Rep was another ex-Tony Crook car, the Mk. II with which he replaced the earlier car and used in 1952 as a combined sports and F2 car with a narrower body than standard — known as the banana car from its shape. Owner Brian Heath let me race that one in a VSCC event.

By now all the Le Mans Reps had auxiliary telescopic dampers at the front and this one used a limited slip differential. So on the track it felt very responsive, with initial understeer but the old problem of rear wheel lifting remained; ride firmness wasn't noticeable on the track although overfirm damping could set the wheels pattering outwards. A remote gear linkage was much more positive. The engine was superb, a BS4 with around 140 bhp, and very smooth, singing on to 6000 rpm with a lovely sound. Partly due to some extra power and slightly better brakes the Le Mans Rep Mk. II was two seconds quicker round Club Silverstone than the BMW; in open wheel form it was also somewhat lower in frontal area.

But heretical though it may seem I infinitely preferred my 1955 Sebring, one of only three built, the first appearing in 1954. It was originally owned by Dickie Stoop who had a long association with AFN, having raced a Mille Miglia for several years; then in 1953 he bought what was probably a Mk. II, which used a normal body but with wings that filled in the area between cycle wings and body. This ran well at the 1953 TT in the hands of Wharton and Robb but when Stoop took it over he promptly wrote it off at Goodwood the following week-end. That chassis number 192 was then used for the Sebring built a year and a half later which should have been 205. By this time Stoop knew roughly what the failings of the original design were, so he specified a combined oil/water radiator, wishbone and coil spring front suspension, and the optional de Dion, located not by the A-bracket but by a single upper link and a Panhard rod. Alfin drums were wider with bigger shoes than standard.

Right and opposite: Dickie Stoop's 1955 Frazer Nash Sebring ran at Le Mans three times, gaining 10th place overall in 1955

The Sebring was effectively the development of the Le Mans Rep Mk. II as organisers had decided that cycle wings were too old fashioned for 1954-55; the body was all-enveloping in the same style as the DB3S Aston with big front-wheel cutaways and the driver sat much more inside a wider cockpit; there was even a little boot space, although the spare wheel and a 25-gallon Le Mans tank filled most of that.

A remote control gear lever, adjustable steering column with nice floor-sprouting pedals gave a comfortable position for those no taller than Stoop. This car too had the BS4 engine which worked extremely well, with no problems at all over the 20,000 miles that I owned the car despite a fair amount of racing. It would start easily and trickle along in traffic at 1500 rpm but its best was from 4000 rpm onwards.

Early in its life with me, we took performance figures at MIRA with a fifth wheel, recording 0-60 mph in 8·0 sec, 0-100 mph in 25 sec, while its best standing start ¼-mile in the VSCC Pomeroy Trophy was 15·45 sec.

On the track it was a much more surefooted car than the Le Mans Replicas, although lowering and stiffening can improve these. Normally you could brake strongly—fade was rare—turn in with some feelable understeer, and then power through the latter part of the corner making sure the inside wheel didn't start spinning; if it did too much, the sudden torque drop would unlock the drive-shaft splines and steer the back-end into a quick wriggle which wasn't always easy to catch cleanly. I never spun it but had some uncomfortable moments. Were it a pure racer one could have stiffened everything up to avoid this, but it was such an enjoyable road car that I didn't want to destroy that attraction.

The ride wasn't particularly good with bronze bushed wishbones, and you learnt to steer round potholes, but at speed it was quite comfortable on fair roads despite racing tyres. The full-width screen protected quite well although rain would creep round it and also attack round the back; the hood was just there for downpours while stationary.

On the track my best ever times with the Sebring were 1 min 14·5 sec at Silverstone and 57·5 sec at the long Prescott hill-climb. By contrast the BMW did 1 min 17·9 sec and 58·5 sec, but the hill-climb suited the BMW better as the Frazer Nash understeered too much on the hairpins.

Having owned the prototype and the last word in post-war Frazer Nash development, I have had the best of both worlds. The BMW Mille Miglia was very advanced for its time—Tyrer used to beat most of the Le Mans Reps in their day—and the Sebring carried on with a tenth at Le Mans in 1955 and winning the *Autosport* championship in 1959; it too was very effective in its day.

Following pages: the author in the ex-Dickie Stoop Frazer Nash Sebring

Ferrari 225S

Enzo Ferrari is a racing man. Brought up in the 1920s and 1930s era of long distance sports and Grand Prix races, where his Scuderia Ferrari works team of Alfa Romeos enjoyed many successes, he appreciated the virtues of fast and reliable engines. It might be unkind to comment, but not untrue, that for the first ten years a Ferrari was an engine, a superb engine, in an unremarkable chassis clothed by some of an artistic country's finest purveyors of the art of coachbuilding; but these cars set the name of Ferrari as a manufacturer on the ladder of fame.

Leaving Alfa Romeo in a huff at the end of 1938, Ferrari founded Auto Avio Costruzione in Modena as sub-contract engineers, but was soon back in racing with his 815 which made its first and only works appearance in that 1940 Mille Miglia. The war saw Ferrari involved in machine tools, expanding to larger premises in nearby Maranello. After the war, machine tools were rapidly elbowed aside and Ferrari car manufacture started with competition as its life force.

His first move was to call his friend Colombo back from Alfa Romeo, where he had originally served under Jano, to design a V-12 for Grand Prix and sports cars. The aim was to beat the Alfetta with its supercharged straight-8 which both men knew well. The V-12 configuration was known to both from Alfa days; they reckoned that its high piston area for little weight per component was the way to go in the search for smoothness and reliability at the high revs they would need to overcome extra rotational and friction losses. A short stroke would keep the engine height down and the casting complexity which might deter others was no problem in Modena, where aluminium foundries were well established. The 60 degree V-12 had bore and stroke of 55×52.5 mm, 124·7 cc per cylinder, giving a capacity of 1497 cc, hence the 125 model number. Two valves per cylinder were operated by chain driven single cams with rockers and hairpin valve springs. Using three downdraught Weber 32DCF carburettors and twin magnetos—one per camshaft—it produced around 100 bhp at 7000 rpm on an 8·5:1 compression ratio. This was mated to a five-speed gearbox with an overdrive fifth. The chassis was an oval tube construction, cross-braced, with unequal length wishbones on needle rollers sprung by an underslung transverse leaf. At the rear, a live axle was used with a normal leaf spring with additional location from the upper trailing arms at the ends of a transverse anti-roll bar; this was an ingenious application providing a facility for adjustable handling that probably wasn't appreciated.

Bodies for the 125 sports cars were Spider Corsa, narrow cigar-shaped two-seaters with cycle wings

The 1949 Le Mans winner, the Ferrari 166M of Chinetti-Selsdon, leading a 3-litre Delage through the glades of the Esses

although one used all-enveloping coachwork. These were reasonably successful in Italian events during 1947. By the end of that year Aurelio Lampredi had returned to Maranello after a brief earlier spell a year before when work on cars had hardly started. Already the 125 had grown to 159 with 59 × 58 mm (158·6 cc per cylinder, 1903 cc). It was Lampredi who was to refine Colombo's basic designs, and also develop the GP unit from a 230 bhp single-stage supercharger single cam to two-stage twin cam layout and 280 bhp.

For 1948 though, Ferrari wanted a 2-litre unit for sports car classes that were being divided at 2000 cc rather than 1500 cc, and for the new Formula 2. Hence the 166 came into being with the bore increased to 60 mm and the stroke later standardised at 58·8 mm to give 166·25 cc per cylinder and 1995 cc. In sports form this gave 150 bhp at 7000 rpm on a compression ratio of 8·5:1 with the F2 unit at 10:1 compression giving 160 bhp. The Spider-bodied cars doubled as F2 competitors. Biondetti won the 1948 Targa Florio with an Allemano-bodied 166 with full-width coachwork and with a GT-bodied car took the 1948 Mille Miglia. And it was a 166 that was to win at Le Mans the following year.

Although there were Spider 166 bodies, it was on the 166 that Vignale produced the famous 'Barchetta' (little boat) that was to become so familiar on the AC via the Tojeiro–Bristol.

The year 1950 also saw the 195 with a 65 mm bore and 160 bhp from 2341 cc. Came the 212 for 1951 with no more power for the road cars but

200 bhp from the 2½-litre GP version. The next year saw the 225 Sport with 70 mm bore and 2715 cc giving 210 bhp at 7200 rpm on a 8·5:1 compression ratio, now with triple 36DCF Weber carburettors. Throughout this rapid growth of model numbers there had been various types of body, usually by Vignale, with different states of engine tune and minor variations in wheelbase.

A particular 225S bought by the American Tom Cole was unusual in that it used a 340MM chassis, 10 cm longer than the normal 225S and with its tubes wider apart round the cockpit area before narrowing for the rear part of the frame. Its rear suspension used upper and lower leaf springs on each side which is a slightly cumbersome arrangement, but may well be kinder to the rear of the chassis in coping with axle wind-up.

Cole took the car to the Targa Florio in 1952 where he came 11th; at Boreham he was third to Parnell's Aston and Salvadori's Ferrari 225. At the Goodwood 9-hour race he co-drove with Graham Whitehead and they finished second to the Collins/Griffith Aston DB3; and its final competition outing was back in Italy at Bari where Cole finished second between Landi and Castelotti, both in 225s.

It would seem that Cole had been learning gradually in the less powerful 225, as the following year he bought a 340MM which gave him a fourth in the Mille Miglia, a second to Hawthorn's similar car at BRDC Silverstone, but at Le Mans, co-driving with Chinetti, he lost his life in an accident at the White House having run as high as third in the first three hours.

Ferrari 166 Spider Corsa could double as an offset single-seater or a sports car, but was no beauty in either form. This scene is Watkins Glen in 1951 . . .

Meanwhile the 225 had been sold to be used as a road car. Peter Gibson acquired it in 1967, some three owners later and in rather tatty condition. It took him five years to strip and rebuild the car completely and, when I tried it in 1972, it was immaculate in every detail; apart from twin-circuit braking and a slightly lower compression ratio it was in 1952 condition.

Somehow one expects those early Ferraris to be uncomfortable, exaggerating the long arm/short leg design of the average Italian; but this one wasn't. A vertical back rest and a large steering wheel with its top almost on the sight line were minor inconveniences but not uncomfortable. A painted metal dash looks very unyielding in today's safety terms.

All this was forgotten as we set out. There was a superb view out across the long red bonnet, under which the thrashing sounds of a triplex cam drive were plainly audible despite the rush of wind around the wrap-round perspex screen, lowered in the centre as a concession to frontal area.

Despite a high specific output—74 bhp/litre— and the smoky tendency for oil to get down the exhaust guides, the engine was perfectly happy whuffling along at 1200 rpm in fifth gear—25 mph. The gearbox uses constant mesh gears with face dogs with the ratios getting closer as they get higher until fifth is only about 10 per cent higher than fourth. It uses the Alfa pattern with fifth in the overdrive position, so you have to move your hand pretty fast through to fifth or the revs drop too

much. The chassis felt pretty good, rigid with no scuttle shake, but the ride was a little bouncy at low speed; faster, and it settled down on the road, responsive almost nervously to the helm, the Avon Turbospeeds starting to slide under power out of sharp corners. It felt as though it would be more at home on the Appenine passes than on the high speed swerves of the main roads in northern Italy, particularly if they were bumpy. Braking was heavy but effective as the large diameter Alfin-type drums have a useful leverage, and Ferrari still eschewed discs.

With a 2·7-litre engine it seemed a well balanced car. In 1952 with a 3-litre 250S Ascari lapped Le Mans at 107·6 mph on 230 bhp; with 70 bhp more in the basically similar 4·5-litre 375 with only another 112 lb he clocked 112·9 mph in 1953; the next year with the 4·9-litre 375 Plus giving 330 bhp Gonzales increased this to 117·5 mph recording a Mulsanne maximum of 160 mph. That another 70 bhp only added 5·3 mph on a circuit where maximum speed is all-important suggests that the bigger-engined versions were cars for the brave— the Pomeroy formula relating power to lap times would have suggested nearer 11 mph. Perhaps Ferrari realised this with the 375 Plus, as that was fitted with a de Dion rear suspension.

However those early 1950s Ferraris had their own charm; their engines were magnificent and sounded glorious and they put the marque firmly on the sporting ladder, but with over 300 bhp available by the end they were an engine in search of a chassis.

Jaguar C-type

Somehow the C-type has never had the same cachet as the D-type; it was technically just as interesting and won Le Mans straight out of the box; it was almost as accelerative and therefore even more remarkable for its day, and it looks very much a Jaguar. So why the lack of the same adulation, reflected in current values and the almost total absence of any C-type from the historic racing scene? It has to be, purely and simply, style and styling—the rounded bluff versus the wind-tunnel elegance. *Motor*, giving the car its first write-up after Le Mans in 1951, dismissed the C-type's style '...mechanical features are allied to a very sleek but workmanlike body, the entire front of which is hinged forward of the front axle and can be swung up complete with lamps for front-end maintenance. Similarly, the complete tail is readily detachable to give access to the rear axle and suspension.

The C-type was conceived purely to win Le Mans, with work starting only eight months or so before the event. In 1950 a trio of XK120s had been run at Le Mans under factory scrutiny; the fastest of these, driven by Leslie Johnson/Bert Hadley, had been as high as second place after 15 hours, at which point it was ahead of the Talbot that eventually won. But they had slipped back to fourth by the time the clutch gave out, overworked through drivers conserving ailing drum brakes uncooled by pressed-steel wheels.

In just about every respect that the XK120 had been a standard production car, so the potential was obviously there to win in 1951 with just a little attention to every department—a bit more power, more roadholding, more brakes and a slightly more slippery shape.

The braking system remained basically XK120 drum brakes but incorporated self-adjustment on the front and cooling air was able to get to them—or heat away—via spoked wheels, which had the added virtue of quick change centre lock hub nuts.

In standard form the XK120 3·4-litre engine gave 160 bhp at that time with the special equipment model producing 180 bhp at 5300 rpm. Revised camshafts with higher lift and attention to the exhaust side—bigger valves and tract with longer cast manifolds—added nearly 20 bhp and a little more for 1952 when the $1\frac{3}{4}$-in SUs were replaced by 2-in carburettors.

The transmission was similar to that of the XK120, with a single-plate 10-in diameter clutch, but the rear axle was of Salisbury manufacture rather than ENV to give greater choice of axle ratios. It was the chassis that was the major novelty which really belied the implication that the C-type was merely a competition version of the XK120. Where the 120 had a refined X-braced twin-channel chassis the C-type used a space frame. Its lower level consisted of 2-in diameter tubing, narrowing

On its way to the first Jaguar Le Mans victory, the stone-chipped C-type of Peter Walker and Peter Whitehead in 1951

D25
1.5 TORCÉ EN VALLÉE
13 MONTFORT LE ROTROU
D 301
CHANTELOUP 4.6
LE MANS 22

between the front wheels and around the engine, and the centre was cross-braced with drilled steel channels each side of the prop-shaft tunnel linked to the outer rail as well as to the cross-members. Its upper level used $1\frac{1}{2}$-in diameter tubes and the struts linking the two were of 1-in section. This fairly rigid basic construction was further torsionally stiffened by a stressed bulkhead at the rear and a stressed scuttle.

At the front upper and lower wishbones with short torsion bars integral with the upper wishbone mounting followed the production design if not its dimensions. Steering, though, was by rack and pinion rather than the production recirculating ball worm and nut.

The rear was more interesting and displayed sound theoretical knowledge. Keeping the chassis as short as possible makes it stiff, so the basic chassis ended just behind the seats and all axle location stemmed from there, unlike the XK120 which used the standard semi-elliptic leaf springs. All the C-type had was just three links—a pair of under-slung trailing radius arms, consisting of steel sheet, and an upper A-bracket with its base on the axle. The subtlety was the placing of the A-bracket offset to the driver's side; in side view the lower and upper links would meet more or less under the gearbox and thus act exactly like a torque tube, loading the rear axle under acceleration by the amount of force that tends to lift the front end of the tube as the pinion tries to climb the crownwheel. In doing this climbing act, the pinion is also lifting weight from the right and transferring it to the left, hence one wheel spins on take-off more easily than the other. By offsetting the point of action of the 'torque-tube force' to an appropriate point on the axle you can eliminate the wheelspin tendency. In fact the amount of offset in relation to half the track is a function of the final-drive ratio; so in theory there should be a different point on the axle for each ratio, but Jaguar overcame this by putting the A-bracket base on the axle to cover the right positions for most likely ratios. This improved traction from a standing start and out of corners although it obviously could not overcome the effects of weight transfer induced by cornering force, and the roll centre was rather high for that.

Springing for the rear axle was also mounted across the rear bulkhead and was a transverse torsion bar, clamped at its centre, joining the trailing arm mounting points. The effect of these steel spring plates is to increase spring rate with body roll; this, in combination with the high roll centre rather undermined the clever location concept, and a limited slip differential was still useful.

And the body so elegantly wrapped around all this machinery was a surprising 28 per cent more efficient in terms of drag factor multiplied by frontal area than the XK120 in Le Mans trim with an aero screen.

Needless to recall, Jaguar won at Le Mans in 1951 with the Walker/Whitehead car taking over from Moss/Fairman whose early pace had decimated the opposition. It nearly did the same for Jaguar as well, as the Moss/Fairman car and that driven by Johnson/Biondetti both suffered fracture of an oil pipe. Although it was a wet race the Jaguar's average speed of 93·5 mph was a new record, as was Moss's fastest lap at 105·2 mph.

Moss also won the 1951 TT with a C-type, so the first season boded well for the new car. However Le Mans 1952 was to be a disaster; the threat of the new Mercedes led Jaguar to try to gain more speed with a revised shape. That was effective enough and they reduced the drag factor by some 26 per cent, but in rearranging the cooling system around the more angled bonnet the header tank became separated from the radiator by too small a pipe and the resultant overheating showed that the water pump design too was defective; so all cars retired with ruined engines before four hours were up. It was a pity because the cars were as reliable as ever once the system had been sorted out, but the body design wasn't adopted for 1953 as it was generating too much lift at the back end, making the cars unstable.

So Le Mans 1953 saw the cars return looking substantially the same, but they were lighter in body, frame gauge and in many other areas. With triple Webers instead of twin 2-in SUs they were also slightly more powerful and torquier; matching this was a new triple-plate clutch of $7\frac{1}{4}$-in diameter rather than the 10-in single dry plate unit, to keep down centrifugal loading.

At the rear, the suspension had been modified to lower the roll centre with a Panhard rod, so the upper fore-and-aft location was provided by a single link which, in theory, should have been adjustable across the axle as it acted on a rod between the two original mounting points for the A-bracket, but I've never seen reference to such adjustment.

And then there were the disc brakes that the C-type made famous; first raced in the Mille Miglia these were the Dunlop multi-pot caliper discs with a prop-shaft driven Girling pump providing additional brake line pressure.

Le Mans 1953 saw Jaguar finish first, second and fourth with the winning Rolt/Hamilton car averaging 105·8 mph, having led from the second hour onwards, apart from a brief period when the Ascari/Villoresi $4\frac{1}{2}$-litre Ferrari took over before its clutch gave up; it was the Ferrari that took fastest lap at 112·9 mph, despite still retaining drum brakes. Although C-types did well at other circuits, it was Le Mans they were built for, so I have concentrated on their performance there, but the first year of the World Sports Car Championship saw Jaguar second to Ferrari with 27 points to 30 without really trying.

Both the C-types I have driven were also tried on the road but that was almost as much their element as on the circuit; chronologically in terms of testing, my first was OVC915 then owned by Rupert Glydon. It had started life being used as the 1953 Le Mans practice car and was then prepared for the Carrera Panamericana; it didn't take part and was sold to Duncan Hamilton at the end of that year. Victory at the Montlhéry Coupe de Paris, at Aintree and several placings were taken in 1954 before the car was sold to Dan Margulies who raced it

C-type revisited, as 1953
24-hour race winners
Tony Rolt and Duncan
Hamilton return to Le
Mans in 1978

regularly at home and abroad. Rupert Glydon acquired it in 1967.

When I tried it in 1971 its engine had grown to 3·8-litres with D-type head specification and it had 62,000 miles on the clock. It also had a D-type gear-box with the Plessey pump brake servo. It certainly went as well as one might expect a sports-racing Jaguar to do, with a lovely Jaguar bark changing to a bellow beyond 3000 rpm; it had been timed over a standing quarter-mile at 13·0 sec and previous owner, Frank Sowden, had clocked 153 mph at Jabbekke, so it was pretty quick. Its gearbox wasn't any quicker on the change for being a D-type as a double declutch, even on the upward change, proved beneficial to smoothness.

What I didn't like at all was the driving position which must have been fairly similar to that in 1953 as the rear bulkhead precludes rearwards adjust-ment; the seat was too high and too close to the steering wheel, so that feet were all wrong for the pedals and it was difficult to heel and toe. It surprised me that drivers could survive their stints in a Le Mans 24-hour race. A nominal full-width perspex screen of vestigial height made it pretty windy too, and I wasn't too impressed by the bumpy jiggly ride, so I decided that it wasn't as good a road car as made out by those who used to drive them to circuits.

However in fairness this car had been set up for historic racing, so the damping was probably firmer than it used to be and someone had given the front wheels negative camber. This didn't affect the ride but it made it a difficult car to drive; an over-responsive front end and a back end that seemed to have some steering effect—it shouldn't have—combined to produce a car that was difficult to place accurately, and cornering tended to follow the line of a 50p piece as steering wheel movements fought against power-variable rear wheel steering. Once this was sorted out it became easier to keep the power firmly on and balance it on the steering, in

which case it all seemed very controllable, but it didn't inspire confidence initially.

In fact my next C-type acquaintance rather confirmed the over-racing set-up of OVC 915. This was the car that used to be MDU 212 and was the fifth to be built, being owned by Tommy Wisdom and Bill Cannel; Wisdom had driven it into sixth place in the 1952 Monaco GP, the car having been previously driven in the 1952 Mille Miglia by Moss/ Dewis with the then experimental disc brakes. It was then driven at the post-Le Mans Rheims sports-car race by Moss and won at 98·2 mph.

In 1954 it was bought by Brig. Michael Head who used it throughout that year, including an epic four-race Swedish trip with no tender car and victory each time. By the time I came to drive it, it had been with Tony Wood for many years and the disc brakes had been converted back to drums at some stage. It was also on Pirelli Cinturatos which may have made all the difference because the car wasn't nearly as nervous as the later one, cornering really quite smoothly. With twin SUs it wasn't as powerful as either, but it felt much more as I would have expected—a fast road car just like an Aston DB3S or a Frazer Nash.

Looking back I see I described the handling in 1971 ... 'you went round in a series of arcs none of which quite tied up with the radius of the corner.' The following year *Road and Track* reported of the ex-Jim Hall XKC 015 ... 'in a series of arcs, no one of which quite matches the radius of the curve ... the C-type must be forced beyond this, by entering each turn at maximum velocity and loading both ends of the car to their extremes. Then the car steered with power and it all works well.'

So it would seem that I wasn't alone in my criticism of the C-type suspension (nor even in the choice of words); but despite that it was effective when driven hard and set Jaguar on the D-type Le Mans trail that was to stand them in such good stead for many years.

Jaguar D-type

To anyone remotely interested in racing of the 1950s the Jaguar D-type is the archetypal sports-racing car, the ultimate in svelte looks which were to live on into the E-type, and the ultimate in its superbly developed engine which could power the cars for so long, make them so fast, and which is still in production over 30 years on from its first appearance. The fact that three companies have produced replicas of the D-type, none exact, is its own endorsement of imitation being the sincerest form of flattery. Equally flattering to the original designers must be the high prices that the cars now command.

The D-type was built unashamedly for Le Mans in days when the rules were vague on the subject of prototypes, and a win in the 24-hour race attracted front page coverage in the national papers. Having won there with the C-types in 1951 and 1953 Jaguar were expected to continue waving the British flag. The result became the D-type, but was far from being just a rebodied C-type, which was basically the state of the C/D prototype that had recorded nearly 180 mph at Jabbekke in October 1953.

Backbone of the D-type was its monocoque centre section in a magnesium alloy; this took the form of a semi-elliptic bottom section from the rear bulkhead to the front wheel, integral with a shorter top section from front bulkhead to rear bulkhead in which holes were cut for driver and passenger. To this was bolted a complex sub-frame with convergent bottom rails running from the front end to the rear bulkhead, with parallel upper rails from the

Unforgettable duel, D-type driven by Hawthorn versus Mercedes 300SLR driven by Fangio in the early stages of the 1955 Le Mans 24-hour Race

front to the front bulkhead, from which tubes angled down to the lower rail. Spread over the top of this was an A-frame running from a point ahead of the longitudinal rails back to the bulkhead edges triangulated back down to the lower rail. On the earlier cars this magnesium tube frame was welded to the front of the tub, but by 1955 the production cars had a strut frame bolted throughout, which made for easier repair.

The sub-frame carried all the front suspension, engine and gearbox, while the rear suspension was completely carried on the rear of the tub. Instead of what might be termed quite a normal system with four links and a lower A-bracket, the D used $\frac{1}{4}$-in thick plates for the trailing arms; although the upper one was carried on rubber bushes, the lower was bronze bushed and could immediately act in torsion with body roll; the upper one would also contribute to this once the rubber had been compressed. These trailing links formed a parallelogram with the A-bracket location chosen not to disturb this geometrically; underslung, it kept the roll centre low, but the torsion plates gave increasing roll stiffness adding to the transverse torsion bar joining the two lower links, and fastened at its centre to give two half-width torsion bars, in effect.

The front suspension used forged wishbones with the upper carrying a torsion bar splined at its forward end into the sub-frame and into the rear arm of the wishbone. This was supplemented by an anti-roll bar linked to the lower wishbone. Dampers all round were telescopic.

Braking followed on from the C-type, with Dunlop six-pot calipers at the front (individual round pads were later replaced by a quick change single pad per side). At the rear four-pot calipers were used. Servo assistance was provided by a Plessey pump driven from the back of the gearbox, increasing hydraulic pressure rather than adding to leverage in the normal vacuum servo layout.

With the engine, Jaguar had a superb start in the C-type unit, which gave around 225 bhp at 5600 rpm with its 40DCO Webers. But there was room for improvement and particularly to the centre of gravity; so dry sump lubrication with the much shallower catch-pan let the engine come down by $2\frac{3}{4}$-in. The scavenge and pressure pumps were driven from the nose of the crank on a worm drive with the dry sump tank at the left-hand rear of the engine compartment—the exhaust side, but an oil cooler was also fitted alongside the radiator.

Increased power came from bigger inlet valves and 45DCO Webers. The C-type valve angles at 35 degrees to the vertical were retained with exhaust at $1\frac{5}{8}$ in while inlets went to $1\frac{7}{8}$ in; in that form the 3442 cc 'six' gave around 245 bhp at 5770 rpm. Increasing inlets by $\frac{1}{32}$ in and exhaust by $\frac{1}{16}$ in, with lift up from $\frac{3}{8}$ in to $\frac{7}{16}$ in, put the 1955 works cars up to 270 bhp at 5500 rpm; the exhaust valve angle had to be increased to 40 degrees to get the bigger inlets in and avoid the risk of touching—hence the wide angle. With inlets up to 2 in, the 1956 cars were up to 277 bhp at 6000 rpm; the following year, a fuel-injected 3·8-litre was giving 306 bhp at 5500 rpm, with torque increased proportionately. Most of the

D-types one sees around on the historic circuits now are using wide-angle engines on 3·8-litre blocks, which give something like 285 bhp. The best Jaguar ever saw from the basic XK engine was on the 1964 alloy-block engine used by Peter Lindner's E-type which, on the same bore and stroke with fuel injection gave a massive 344 bhp at 6500 rpm. In fact you can get 2-in inlets into the wet-sump 3·8-litre, but all Jaguar outputs were based on the need to run for 24 hours whereas even a hectic historic season might only cover six hours including testing.

A D-type gearbox is another unique feature with synchromesh on bottom gear inside a new casing. And, although a crank damper was fitted at the front, there was no separate flywheel, the starter ring being part of the clutch housing, hence the D-type starter motor mounted on top of the gearbox.

Wheels too were novel. Where the C-type had knock-off wire-wheels on splined hubs, the search for lightness and more guaranteed quick change capabilities led to an aluminium centre, drilled for air to get away from the disc brakes, with an aluminium or steel nose-piece bolted to it, the bolt heads acting as pegs on the back to engage on the hub flange. Rims were also aluminium, of $5\frac{1}{2}$-in width. Although the wheel arch enclosed part of the wheel, quick-lift jacks acting on the monocoque allowed the wheels to descend far enough to be removed with only slight angling for the rear.

All this magnificent Browns Lane engineering was wrapped in Malcolm Sayer's all-time greatest shape, smooth, shapely and with no aerodynamic afterthoughts, other than the fin designed to move the centre of pressure rearwards for high speed stability in cross-winds. Works cars grew longer noses in 1955 for improved high speed penetration, but customer cars and production XKSS kept the blunter variety. Le Mans regulations over the years forced a change from the wrap-round aero, followed by the full-wrap-round back to the fin, and then full-width (and taller) for 1956.

It is interesting to look at the maximum speeds recorded by the various Jaguars at Le Mans since the organisers started timing them at Les Hunaudières (beyond this point some speeds are still increasing). In 1953 the fastest C-type clocked 152 mph; the 1954 D-type immediately took that up to 172·8 mph. Another 10 per cent horsepower put that to 175·2 mph in 1955. Come the 1956 full width screen, and speed dropped to 156·9 mph, but the extra power of the 1957 Hamilton 3·8-litre put this back to 178·3 mph, a speed that was equalled in 1962 by the 5-litre Maserati coupe but not beaten until 1964, although Ireland did go faster in practice with the Aston P214 in 1963. Some of this was a function of the 3-litre sports limit, but GTs and later experimental cars (1962) were allowed bigger engines, so the speed is a considerable tribute to Sayer's 1954 shape.

Over the years I have driven three D-types, two of them by courtesy of Anthony Bamford, and the third run in the JCB championship. They all have that same feel of lovely cars perfectly put together,

as at home on the open road as on the track, and they can easily be driven to the circuits without fluffing plugs or even suffering from an overfirm ride. The only feature that was a function of all three and which I didn't like is the tendency to lift the inside rear wheel and get it spinning despite a limited slip differential. I found it less noticeable on the circuits, except on tighter corners. In some ways it acts as a safety valve, that instant power on the limit isn't going to put the tail straight out, but it does prevent maximum power getting to the road till the car is almost straight. Why does it do it? I'm sure it is a function of too great a build up in rear roll stiffness, and probably applied to some extent with the one-off de Dion application unless that did away with the spring plates and used radius rods. Radius rods and spherical joints should be the answer unless the A-bracket mountings then bring in conflicting geometry.

However the drive I enjoyed most was the day that I raced XKD 512 back in 1970, despite the rain, and the following is an extract from the report in *Motor* of a day to remember. The car was owned by the late Nigel Moores who had set up Speed Merchants to promote historic racing with Bill Allen; it was they who were behind the first historic championship—the JCB.

My car was the black one that Bill Allen normally drove, Bill being given the helm of XKD 606—at least it has the Jaguar 606 stamp on the chassis frame, even though other parts may be elsewhere. Mine was XKD 512 which was sold to Lord Louth as a road car and was subsequently taken out to South Africa where John Love raced it. The other was XKD 515 which Col. Ronnie Hoare kept as a road car until 1961 and even then has only 14,000 miles on the clock! Both are 1955 cars.

Practice on the Saturday was dry and I turned up early to make sure that I was going to fit the car; mechanics Paul Kelly and John Pearson had it warmed up for me to make a familiarisation run up and down the club straight. I fitted quite easily into the cockpit and found everything in easy reach and

the pedals properly spaced although with little room for the clutch foot to do anything but remain poised.

After instructions on appropriate gauge readings I had a quick squirt up the runway *sans* helmet; normally a car feels desperately slow when you aim it down a large runway but this didn't. It's a great 'torquey' engine, particularly with the 3·8-litre engine, but it still gets on song from 3500 rpm onwards with a real shove in the back. With a 5800 rpm rev limit and the slow deliberate Jaguar change it felt as if it would do 0-100 mph in around 12 secs.

By the time practice came I felt reasonably at home in the car; the odd tail slide when U-turning on the runway had shown that the steering was direct and ideally geared to catch any rear-end wander and that the servo discs were really powerful. Inevitably with someone else's expensive motor car I started fairly gently, braking before my normal drum-braked but slower Frazer Nash and using only 5000 rpm. When the pit signals started to appear they said 2 min 5 sec which against a FN best of 1 min 58·5 sec was pretty gentle. However they came down a second at a time without any obvious extra effort until I came in to have the radiator blind lifted. Out again, using the brakes and acceleration to something like their potential, another 4 sec came off before the end and I got down to 1 min 54·2 sec. Not fast enough to get the adrenalin pumping hard but enough to understand the car—Hawthorn with a proper D-headed 3·4 did 1 min 50 sec.

I was using third gear for all the corners except Becketts, taken in second. Top at Woodcote dropped the revs to around 4000 rpm which didn't give the instant throttle response that third did; Hawthorn did the same so I wasn't being chicken!

The fastest part of the circuit down to Stowe saw about 5300 rpm on the clock, around 130 mph. In the corners the attitude was very dependent on throttle position; Copse was rather slippery and the car drifted wide, almost understeering, until the throttle was opened; then the car set itself more

Martin Morris in XKC 404, one of the early 1954 D-types, at Le Mans in 1978. This was the first D-type to win a race, at Reims in 1954 when it was driven by Wharton and Whitehead

Following pages: short-nose D-type with Chris Drake at the helm at the Nürburgring

Long-nose 1957 car beside a Derbyshire lake—it was always a lovely car to drive, apart from its wheelspin

firmly on the road before aiming out of the corner up to Maggots, which wasn't quite flat for a newcomer. For Becketts it was down to second with an easy heel and toe, then a series of little tail slides as the D pivoted around its nose with each flick of the throttle before sorting out the correct attitude; with the throttle squeezed rather than prodded the tail came out gradually after the apex and the well located live axle took the power remarkably early, the throttle a more effective adjunct to the steering wheel than with modern power/tyre ratios.

Down to Stowe, where the brakes had to work hard again, you balance the car with oversteer and aim at a late apex, then out parallel to the grass towards Club for an early apex. The tail comes out slightly again to line up early for Abbey in third, then under the bridge to Woodcote, long and fast with the car balanced neutrally. The blare of sound, the rush of wind, the sight of that long gracefully curved bonnet, the reassuring feel of unurgent power—I could have gone on for ages but respect for other people's machinery and for the chequered flag brought it all to an end.

I was expecting to go a little faster in the race on the Sunday, but it rained. I was given instructions on keeping the engine blipping on the line to keep the plugs clean and then went out on the warming up lap; it wasn't actually raining at the time, although it had done so heavily earlier, but there were puddles everywhere of indeterminate depth.

However, the car still stopped all square and with its narrow Dunlop R6s held a straight line when it was wanted, except when accelerating through one of the deeper puddles.

Then came the race and the rain. The start was all right but as the cars headed for Copse in a wall of spray that completely hid those ahead, I backed off letting the 2-litre Cooper–Bristols and Lotus Xs engulf me; there was no way I was going to risk driving into something I couldn't see. Ahead Neil Corner's Maserati 250F was away like a rocket with Richard Bond in the ex-Gordon Lee Lister and sundry other Listers and Masers, both sports and racing, and the upright 2-litre ERA of Martin Morris in the middle behind them. I had forgotten quite how thick spray could be when thrown up by open wheelers but fortunately if you recognise when the corner is coming up you can see round it as the spray is then going in another direction.

I soldiered on letting the blue D-type through—the long-nose one didn't run as if it was its first post-rebuild race—as well as others I had hoped to beat in the dry. In a masochistic sort of way I enjoyed it and was almost disappointed when the flag came out three laps early. I had finished well down but was thankful to have kept it on the island—some didn't.

So the D was returned with reluctance to its owners who must have accepted it back with relief—brave of them to let me race on a track that wet. It is such a civilised well mannered device, the last of the true racing road cars.

HWM-Jaguar

Doubtless it was the Le Mans-proven reliability, and the ready availability of similar parts from production cars, that attracted special builders to the Jaguar engine, and HWM were really the first to capitalise on the option, once they had been shown the way by a privateer. That private entrant was Oscar Moore, already well known for the OBM that had started life as a BMW 328—the ex-Leslie Johnson GHX 516—and finished up looking rather like an HWM, and proved very effective too.

While Moore was campaigning the OBM, Hersham and Walton Motors, under John Heath and George Abecassis, had been developing pre-war Altas and then running 1948 Altas, Abecassis in single-seater form and Heath with a slab-sided streamliner built up on a pre-war frame for sports-car racing. For 1949, though, HWM built new 1½-seaters to double as Formula B single-seaters without wings and 2-litre sports-cars, using the Alta engine for both.

The chassis was developed Alta, using wishbones with Standard uprights and lower transverse leaf spring at the front, and a live axle located by trailing quarter-elliptic springs and a single torque arm—foreshadowing the Jaguar C-type. Heath had a good Continental season with the HW-Alta, so

Following pages: Phil Scragg's hill-climb HWM-Jaguar has a wide-angle D-type engine. The coupe behind it was built up by George Abecassis on an HWM-Jaguar chassis *Below:* HWM-Jaguar pit stop by the Marshall-Protheroe car in the 1955 Goodwood Nine Hours. They finished eighth

HWM decided to run a works team of three cars, selling a fourth.

The new cars, called HWM, had redesigned chassis using the same front suspension but replaced the live axle with a wishbone and leaf spring independent rear suspension. The Alta engine was retained and mated to an Armstrong-Siddeley epicyclic gearbox, and the lot was clothed in a neat rounded body with cycle wings when necessary. Abecassis, Moss and Heath had another good Continental season and decided to expand still further for 1951 with no fewer than five single-seaters. So the 1950 cars were sold and Oscar Moore bought the prototype that had been John Heath's regular mount. Moore had one season with XMC 34 in that form and then inserted a Jaguar unit, bored out during that year to 3·8-litres. Phil Scragg also put a Jaguar engine into an HWM chassis in 1952—possibly an HW-Alta chassis as there shouldn't have been a spare 1950 car—and both Moore and Scragg had successful seasons through to 1954, with Scragg concentrating on hill-climbs and sprints.

By this time HWM had had reasonable success in the F2 period of Grand Prix racing and then tried briefly with the 2½-litre, but it had already begun to look as if the new era of GP racing was beyond their limited resources and that sports-car racing could be more rewarding. So the first HWM-Jaguar was built up in the summer of 1953 using a chassis similar to that of the F2 cars but with transverse leaf and wishbone at the front with a de Dion tube at the rear located by four links and a sliding peg—the rear end location had been adopted on the single-seaters after early attempts with splayed quarter-elliptics and a single radius arm as a development of that on the HW-Alta. Rear end springing was by longitudinal torsion bars. Braking was provided by dual circuit hydraulics operating with large Alfin-type drums, inboard at the rear.

Three such cars seem to have been built, HWM 1 and later XPA 748 and VPA 9 under an aluminium all-enveloping skin reminiscent of Heath's original slab-sided HW-Alta but with a larger intake. Late 1953 had seen Heath going well in the 9-hour race and Abecassis winning a sports-car race at September Goodwood. For 1954, HWM returned to the Continental scene although the Mille Miglia with Abecassis driving saw a broken shock absorber retire the car. Abecassis managed to beat the DB3S Astons and the Ecosse C-types at the wet International Trophy to finish second behind Gonzales' big Ferrari, a result repeated in Sweden later behind d'Oliveira's Ferrari. Rheims saw an HWM now fitted with coil springs and double wishbones like the F2 cars and seventh place for Whitehead/Gaze, with Gaze taking XPA 748 to a Crystal Palace victory. HWM 1 managed fourth on scratch in the Dundrod TT that year, 14th on handicap.

For 1955, three more chassis were built, one eventually to become a roadgoing coupe while the others became HWM 1 (again) and XPE 2 under more curvaceous bodies. There were fewer outings for these but the Goodwood 9-hours saw Macklin/Smith take fourth overall in XPE 2. For 1956 these two cars were given the latest 3·4-litre D-type engines complete with drum sump lubrication, and Abecassis finished second to Moss' DB3S in the International Trophy meeting. But John Heath wanted to do the Mille Miglia again and took a car which would appear to have been the first HWM 1; sadly he crashed and died in hospital and that was really the end for HWM as a racing company. The cars were sold to private hands in 1957 and all survive bar VPA 9 (perhaps the Heath accident car)

The comfortable cockpit of the HWM-Jaguar makes it an acceptable road car. Note the gear lever behind the D-type box

including the car that Phil Scragg used to replace his earlier car—a new two-seater sports chassis with cycle wings and a wide-angle dry sump D-type engine, registered SPC 982, assembled in 1959.

The one I came to drive was the second HWM 1. This had been used by Noel Cunningham-Reid and then John Bekaert before he took to Lister–Jaguars. Richard Bond found it in 1973, using it in historic racing before selling it to Kirk Rylands.

Close inspection of HWM machinery showed it to be very well built with some fine detail work. It was interesting to see that the de Dion tube was split in the middle to allow separate rotation of the two halves, which would be necessary if the trailing arms weren't equal or parallel.

It is always nice to get behind a racing Jaguar engine. It is an appealing piece of machinery whatever chassis it is in; in a light-weight space frame like that of the HWM the response to the throttle is rather more electrifying than in a D-type, which was built for the long distance endurance races, whereas the HWM feels as though it were built for the sprints and adapted for longer events. The driving position isn't too comfortable for a start with the bent knees and long arms of the Italians, but it is still easy enough to drive and place accurately even if the gear lever is rather farther from the steering wheel than is ideal for comfort.

Unfortunately the Silverstone Club circuit was well saturated when I came to try the car. Inevitably I couldn't really use the full power/weight ratio to advantage in the conditions, but it was certainly very quick in a straight line and seemed to put its power down well once the line was straight trouble was, that it seemed never to have been sorted to best advantage, which is surprising, really, when people like John Bekaert used to campaign the car so effectively—or perhaps it had just got a little tired since then.

Given the basic chassis and suspension specification, it should have handled quite well, but the suspension travel at the rear was so limited by over-stiff springing that the ride was poor, while the power oversteer was almost instantaneous. The

back was ready to step out of line whenever power was even partly applied, and when it started to slide half-way through Maggots on a steady throttle, I felt that discretion was certainly the better part of valour. In fairness, the conditions had become very wet but I didn't feel the car was helping. Owner Kirk Rylands appeared to feel much the same about the car, but assumed that, since it was as driven by Bekaert and, more recently, Richard Bond, it was up to him to learn to cope with it.

For all my up-bringing, I am not so great a respecter of the past that I think nothing should be adjusted where adjustability is, in fact, built in; to start with, the car has anti-roll bars both ends, which implies some adjustment and the rest can be done on spring rates, damper settings and sundry angles. With such limited rear suspension travel I wanted softer springing and possibly softer damping at the back, but Kirk took the problem to a tame chassis expert who attacked it at the other end with a stiffer front anti-roll bar. On a smooth circuit the effect should be much the same, but at the time of writing similar lap times have been achieved with considerably less effort.

Perhaps it was largely due to the response of the engine to the throttle, with good lusty torque almost anywhere in the rev range, but it would have been a real handful, with a more peaky engine in the wet. At the other end of the rev scale it is an impressively tractable unit, able to potter along in top at about 30 mph—an ideal racing/touring unit as Kirk discovered when using the car to drive to Phoenix Park for a historic race meeting.

In other respects the car was very well prepared, looking as well as if not better than it did when new. The steering was nice and precise and very quick, which was probably essential, but since then Kirk has fitted the original larger steering wheel to give slightly more arm movement for a given lock.

Back in the pits I took a retrospective hat off to the past protagonists of the car, but I would like to have another go in the dry with the suspension adjustment. Given better brakes there should be little reason for it to be much slower than a Lister-Jaguar.

Maserati 300S, 450S and Tipo 61

Blood-red, beautiful and awesome in its noise, the car on the far side of the circuit was in its element; the rise and fall of that baying bark wafting across the field told its own story of straights and corners, brakes and cornering, man and machine enjoying life—it was the song of the Trident. As the 300S came towards us the deep bark, harsher than a Jaguar's, grew in volume; just opposite, the note dropped a few decibels as the nose dipped, there was a quick blip of sound, the bonnet lifted again as the driver accelerated through the climbing right hander, back on full song and away up the hill, with the upward change producing a scarcely discernible drop in note. It could have been any mid-1950s circuit, but it was the welcome herald to another track test, albeit on a borrowed airfield perimeter track.

I tried the big brother 450S three years later at Snetterton, and the successor to both, the 2·8-litre 'Birdcage' Tipo 61, five years earlier around a private estate. So with no direct circuit comparisons we'll have to stick to chronology.

Just as the Maserati 250F developed from the A6GCM 2-litre Formula 2 car, so too did the 300S come from experience on the sporting A6GCS, itself a 1952 development of the original 1947 two-seater. The A6 cars used a six-cylinder engine with a four-speed gearbox attached to it. A tubular frame carried double wishbone and coil springs at the front, with a live axle at the rear located by radius arms and A-bracket, and sprung on quarter elliptics. In 1954 a couple of cars ran with the $2\frac{1}{2}$-litre GP engine and were labelled as 250S, but in neither the Mille Miglia nor the Supercortemaggiore Monza 1000 Km race did they last the distance. With the 250F well under way during 1954, the 300S was shown at the end of 1954, along with the little 150S, a scaled down version for regular customer sale.

The 300S was very much a two-seater version of the 250F. The six-cylinder all-alloy engine with dry liners had twin overhead camshafts driven by spur gears, and used dry sump lubrication. Where the 250F used 84 × 75 mm dimensions, the 300S had a 90 mm stroke for 2993 cc and something like the same power, but more torque on triple Webers.

Maserati 300S poised for a track test

Maserati 450S No. 4509
in definitive form, as a
compact and powerful
V-8

The 300S mounted its oil tank alongside the fuel tank rather than behind it, as in the 250F's pointed tail.

The chassis too followed the same layout with track and wheelbase almost identical, although the overall length of the 300S was some 4 in greater; the frame used twin upper and lower tubes per side, but extended cross members were used to support the elegant Fantuzzi bodywork wrapped around a lattice of smaller tubes.

At the front, wishbones and coil springs were familiar, but the rear suspension used a de Dion tube mounted ahead of a combined gearbox/final drive and located by sliding peg and radius arms; springing was via a transverse leaf spring. The transmission was the four-speed 250F unit with its shafts across the car behind the final drive.

The 300S started well in 1955 with third and fourth at Sebring for Spear/Johnson and Valenzano/Perdisa behind Jaguar and Ferrari, but that was all they achieved in championship races in a year which saw the Mercedes 300SLR domination; the Mille Miglia saw the solo entry retire after holding third, while Le Mans saw both retire with transmission trouble, although Musso/Valenzano had run second for some time until retiring in the 20th hour. A fifth at the TT was followed by a broken axle in the Targa Florio.

However non-championship races, even long-distance ones, saw them fare better; third and fourth in Sicily, the first victory at Bari (Behra from Musso's 300S), victory over Ferrari at the Monza 1000 Km (3-litre limit), fourth at the Swedish GP and victory for Fangio in Venezuela.

Good though the 300S could be, it just wasn't fast enough, losing 15 mph to the 300SLR Mercedes at Le Mans and 27 mph slower than the big Ferrari. So the end of 1955 saw development on more power with a more substantial chassis—and they were still on drum brakes too. Work proceded on two engines, a 3½-litre six (86 × 100 mm) and a 4½-litre V-8, while the chassis followed 300S principles at the front but changed the rear layout; a new five-speed gearbox had its shaft in-line and in front of the final drive, so the de Dion tube sat behind the assembly and was located by peg sliding in a chassis-mounted slot; it was driven by drop gears from the clutch housing behind the engine. While the 3½-litre engine followed the 300S in basic design it used different castings and subsequently formed the basis of the roadgoing unit. The V-8 was obviously a different kettle of fish altogether.

It was designed for confrontation with Ferrari to start at 4½-litres and be capable of enlargement—later to as much as 6·4-litres for speedboat use. Dimensions of 93·8 × 81 mm were chosen for 4477 cc. Twin cams per bank had valves operated by roller-follower rockers and restrained by hairpin valve springs. Twin magnetos fed dual plugs per cylinder and four Webers sat in the middle of the vee to give around 400 bhp at 7200 rpm.

The first round of the 1956 championship saw the 300S team acquit themselves well with Moss winning at Buenos Aires, but fifth was the best they could do at Sebring for which a 350S arrived, but was not used. Moss used the new car in the Mille Miglia but found the front end poor and prone to lift, finally crashing in the rain; neither of the 300S finished. Nürburgring saw victory again for the 300S after Moss/Behra took over the Taruffi/Schell car.

In the aftermath of 1955, the ACO had reduced the Le Mans capacity limit for prototypes (less than 50-off) to 2½-litres and thus excluded their race from the championship, so Maserati missed the event, although a couple of 250F-powered Lago Talbots ran without success. So the final round was the Swedish GP and Maserati brought along a 450S as well as three 300S; the 450S didn't have the brakes or handling in the 350S chassis so wasn't used, and the 300S all failed, two having suffered brake trouble. Despite a poor final showing Maserati finished up second in the championship to Ferrari.

Over the winter new front end suspension geometry and bigger brakes, albeit still drums, were added to the 450S design and Maserati were set to tackle the 1957 sports car championship, as well as the GPs, in earnest.

Buenos Aires saw the redoubtable combination of Moss/Fangio easily leading when the clutch failed; Moss switched to the 300S, took the lap record, and reached second place between a pair of 3½-litre Ferraris. The 450S clocked its first victory at Sebring with Fangio/Behra from Moss/Schell in a 300S. So far so good.

Four cars appeared at the Mille Miglia on home ground—two 450S, a 300S with a 3½-litre V-12 and a 300S; one 450S crashed before the start, Moss covered seven miles before his brake pedal broke, the V-12 holed its sump and the 300S, with the 450S front brakes, scored a fourth behind Ferraris.

Four cars went to Nürburgring, the Mille Miglia combination and a private 300S. Moss led in one 450S until a wheel broke, drove the other until an oil tank came loose, drove one 300S but gave it back because it wasn't handling right, finally finishing fifth with Fangio in the private 300S. Aston beat Ferrari to keep the championship open.

Come Le Mans and Maserati ran a Costin-styled coupe 450S as well as an open one; by the time the coupe had been stabilised, and air scooped to its overheated interior it was no faster than the open car. However the open car led for a short time during the second hour, having completed the first hour behind the 4-litre Hawthorn Ferrari. But then a drive-shaft seized and the car was out. At the time the coupe was second, but eventually suffered the same problem after a stop for a broken oil pipe had dropped them down to near the bottom of the field.

In Sweden the cars fared better and although one 450S suffered the same problem as at Le Mans, Moss/Behra won in the other from the Hill/Collins 4·1-litre Ferrari and a 300S also driven by Moss—he took a turn in the other 450S too.

For the final round in Venezuela victory could lead to the championship so Maserati took two 450S, a V-12 3½-litre and a 300S while Temple Buell had a third 450S, the big cars running with an auxiliary two-speed box aft of the clutch. Against them Ferrari, who also needed victory for the championship, ranged two 4·1-litres and two 3-litres. Gregory in the Temple Buell 450S took the lead in the first lap but rolled the car on the second. Moss had a hesitant start but worked through to the lead when he was chopped at full speed by an amateur AC driver and a second 450S was out. A fire at the pits in the third one was extinguished and Moss tried again only to find the seat was still burning and had to stop; Shell tried this time and was just lapping Bonnier in the 300S, when that had

Charles Lucas puts 4509 through its paces at Silverstone. This car has the 'proper' transmission. *Following pages:* 4509 and 4510

a tyre burst, taking both cars off the road, one to be written off against a lamp post, the other to catch fire—again. And the V-12 didn't start because of a broken transmission, so Ferrari gained a 1, 2, 3, 4 from a local 300S. And with that hideously expensive Keystone Cops performance the Maserati effort came to an end hastened by the arrival of the 3-litre formula for 1958.

Having finally retired from their own racing, Maserati continued development on the V-12 in 3-litre form in the 300S chassis during 1958, but moved on to a 'birdcage' design for the Tipo 60 in 1959 with the 2-litre 'four'. Birdcage described a chassis made up of a multiplicity of small tubes, and must have been designed more by intuition than skill, as it would have needed a computer to stress so many tubes running at different angles, but it was very effective in its light strength further reinforced by some stressed panels. Twin wishbones featured at the front with a de Dion axle at the rear and together with an integral five-speed final drive transaxle were features carried on from before, but the braking system finally used discs all round.

Success with the 2-litre during 1959 led to the stretching of the engine to 2·8-litres for the Tipo 61 and an impressive debut for two of them at Nassau at the end of that year led to the Camoradi team created by Lucky Casner. Although the team managed an occasional non-championship victory, they led every one of the other races in the early stages, even at Le Mans, but only emerged with one championship victory for Moss/Gurney in bad weather at the Nürburgring. It was an identical story in 1961 for the last of the front-engined sports Maseratis; the Tipo 61 again won a wet

Nürburgring, and also at Rheims' non-championship event. But by this time Maserati had produced mid-engined derivatives which were to fare no better; in fact they were worse, and a Maserati was never again to get near the front of a major sports car race, even those that accepted prototypes after the championship went over to GT cars in 1962.

Thus the 450S was the last of the leviathans from Modena, and was ably supported by the more agile 300S, while the Birdcage flattered only to deceive. What then were they like to drive?

Having driven five different Maserati competition cars I can only conclude that all Maseratis are something of a handful, and the Birdcage was the nicest. But I may have been unlucky. All the bigger cars, including a 250F, were really only happy when in the corner with the power down and the attitude balanced on the throttle—understeer just wasn't in the factory vocabulary at the time. A common factor separating the 250F and derivative sports cars from the Birdcage was the steering; the Birdcage used rack and pinion but the others used a worm and sector box with bell-cranks and levers. Apart from that, their basic design layout was identical with wishbone front suspension and de Dion tube apparently well located; but the steering on the big cars was characterised by a dead feeling straight ahead and little feel in the corners—heavy on the 450S; thus the best way for the driver to inform himself of the car's attitude was via the seat of the pants rather than the fingers.

Some of the blame or credit for this must go to Guerrino Bertocchi, Maserati's chief tester from pre-war days, a driver wedded to the marque with probably little experience of other cars; it was acceptable in the hands of such masters of the knife-edge as Fangio and Moss, but accentuated their skill in relation to lesser mortals. If one adds Behra to those and looks at a list of Maserati performances, these three accounted for 72 per cent of 250F victories, 85 per cent for the 300S and all the three 450S victories. That might just be attributed to shrewd team selection, but one can argue that their natural rivals in other cars might not have enjoyed the same success in the Maseratis.

The 300S I tried was 3072 from 1957, fresh out of restoration at PAO in Wiltshire. It is a car you sit in, surrounded by exposed tubes and no trim with minimal instrumentation ahead; the driving position was quite good with straight enough legs and bent arms and a good view over the falling bonnet to place the car accurately.

The gear lever nestled by the left thigh, its precise gate offset on the tunnel. Ratios on the other end were a little difficult to fathom; with 150 mph gearing, bottom was very high, second and third followed quite reasonably, but fourth was so close to third that it was hardly worth a downchange, although the delightfully light movement and the heady noise of the blaring six encouraged its use.

At speed it became immediately apparent that the car was all over the place in a straight line, picking up every surface variation with a weaving that seemed ideally designed to discourage Mille Miglia crowds without help from the driver. And it was bouncy on the corners, so that it was difficult to know if the rear end movement was loss of grip or loss of contact. Sprung to carry a 30-gallon load, it is necessarily firm in the unladen condition, but slackening the rear dampers improved the cornering behaviour considerably, although the steering deadness was still disconcerting on the way into corners. It needed to be braked in a straight line — the drums were quite satisfactory once warm — and powered through the corner during which, at some point, the front wheels would be pointing at the infield; fun in the Appenines but difficult on long high speed corners.

While the 300S was light and felt controllable, the 450S was a heavy brute with stiff heavy steering and ponderous, pendulous oversteer and the front suspension could, with no obvious warning, develop the most appalling shudder at low speed. The V-8 engine was splendid with massive torque but it needed its claimed 400 bhp to accelerate the solid 2360 lb of the car.

The car I tested, 4510, was one of a pair built at the end of 1958 for America; at one stage it had been fitted with a conventional Corvette gearbox and final drive unit to replace a damaged Maserati box. It still had this rather heavy four-speed box, as well as disc brakes that the factory had produced for the car but not actually used at the time. These were pretty heavy, too, which at least made the controls consistent.

In feel it was obviously a 300S derivative in that cornering needed power, but it lacked the sense of controllability of the smaller car and I'm sure it would have been very hard work in a long distance race. Fast and furious it is not a car for the timid.

The Birdcage, though, was a totally different animal — short, sharp and responsive with power-induced slides easily caught. The canted four gives a nice low bonnet line enhancing the feeling of control, and the steering was light and precise with a nice driving position.

The transmission was noisy and rather vaguer in selection than with the 300S four-speed unit, but the ratios seemed to complement the peaky power curve and you were never caught between gears and off the cam. Its engine note didn't have the appeal of the sonorous six or the rumbling V-8 but it was very effective and not too vibratory — a frequent problem on big-pot racing 'fours'.

The Birdcage was arguably Maserati's last great car from their 1950s heyday but was rendered instantly obsolete, not only by the changing shape of sports-car racing, but by the new generation of mid-engined Lotus 19s.

At Le Mans in 1960 the Camoradi Tipo 61 makes a mockery of the wind-screen height ruling

Ferrari 250GT and GTO

The sound under that curvy red bonnet is harsh and urgent, a mechanical cacophany in marked contrast to the refined burr that the onlookers hear, almost the whine of a supercharger, as the GTO accelerates out of the Goodwood chicane, past the pits and away on another lap of the circuit that saw the Italian cars so successful. But the mechanical thrash of valve gear that is so characteristic of front-engined Ferraris no longer fills the cockpit as it seemed to in the cautious opening laps; the adrenalin has taken over, the concentration is all on keeping that bonnet where you want it, little flicks of the big wood-rimmed Nardi wheel tightening the line into the corner, unwinding smoothly to keep the tail in check as the power comes on in response to pressure on a firm and progressive throttle cracking open 12 thirsty Weber chokes.

Madgwick's long right-hander comes up, climbing slightly which seems to increase the understeer; by the time you have taken the apex and come back out to the grass it is time to attack Fordwater so that the two are almost just one long right-hander; a bump on the exit moves the car bodily sideways as you move out again to straight-line the slight kink before the right-handed part of St. Mary's. You don't have to brake too heavily for that, but if you take it too fast you won't get back on the inside of the track for the left-handed dive down St. Mary's dip; better to be cautious and enjoy the tighter corner on the proper line. Steering, which feels rather dead and uninspiring in the straight-ahead position, tells you all you want to know once you have applied some lock and cornering force to the system; you can feel the understeer on the way into a corner—light steering goes lighter still—but you can feel it going even lighter as power is applied to bring the tail out in a classic drift, at which point you are driving by your pants and apply corrective lock, which may or may not be opposite, depending on the speed of the corner and the power surplus available.

Climbing the hill out of St. Mary's you head towards the twin right-handers that make Lavant corner almost a long hairpin, but with the second part almost flat from the apex of the first; the left-hander a third of the way along Lavant straight is again almost flat, now in fourth, before the fast approach to Woodcote, another double right with a fast first part which you try to straight-line under braking, firm positive brakes with a giant hand effect while you drop a couple of ratios, feet dancing on floor-mounted pedals while the right hand steers a massive lever forward into fourth, then back into

third using spring-loading to ensure the correct plane.

Another flick round Woodcote with the tail just sliding, accelerate away, brakes again for the chicane, second if you feel like it, but it will take it in third and away on another lap. The acceleration doesn't actually feel that fantastic to start with, but you soon realise that it only seems unimpressive because the power comes in so smoothly, and it just keeps accelerating up to the 7000 rpm I was using, and probably equally beyond; a good seat helps to mask the effect too.

The inside of a GTO is not designed to subdue the under-bonnet sounds unless it has been trimmed subsequently; this one had painted aluminium sheeting, matt-black to match the instrument surrounds. You can tell it is a racer because it doesn't have a speedometer—just a big rev counter dead ahead through the top of the three-spoked steering wheel (spokes at 2.30, 6.00 and 9.30 on the clock-face) flanked by oil pressure and temperature gauges on the right, fuel pressure and water temperature gauges on the left with a fuel gauge far left.

The driving position is fairly typical of Italian cars of the period; even average-size drivers have to splay their knees because the pedals are too close even when the arms are straight, but you get used to it even when driving on the left of the cockpit.

Its immediate predecessor the 250GT and its successor the 1964 GTO were just the same in driving position; it was only the view but that was a bit different. In feel, the 250GT is certainly heavier and seems much more of a road car, but its basic characteristics of vague steering straight ahead regaining feel once lock is applied, and the control of the tail by the right foot are the same; it is just in tautness and ultimate performance that the GTO feels the better racer. Not surprisingly the 1964 GTO feels like the classic GTO; it is really just a normal GTO rebodied along the lines of the mid-engined LM but with a few detail differences like wider wheels, twin-circuit braking and a better-tuned exhaust system.

A brief run in a 275LM showed a very different kind of car. It is mid-engined and puts the driver particularly far forward. As the front falls away so sharply you just can't see anything solid in front of the screen—you drive along feeling as though your legs are dangling over the edge of a cliff, conscious that a great mass of Ferrari behind might catch up with your toes at the slightest provocation. It didn't and, in fact, felt quite stable at speed, but it isn't a comfortable car to drive, with the pedals well offset

to the inside to avoid the wheel arches. Compared with the GTO, the peak of a vanished era, the LM seemed as if it were making rather faltering steps into the new pool, a tip-toe car that required respect and more grip at the rear. Perhaps I'll feel differently when I try one again, but I wasn't at home.

Ferrari had already built GT cars for road-going customers and for some of the sports-car events before the 250GT lineage was established; the brutal looking 1952 250MM with Farina coachwork was the fastest of that breed. Came 1954 and the long-standing-line of the 250GT was laid down under a skin that closely resembled the 250 Mille Miglia, with its high rounded nose and squat cockpit set well back blending into the nicely rounded tail via a 'fast back'.

In design it followed the basic layout of the original Ferraris, a front-mounted V-12 in a tubular chassis with independent front suspension and a live rear axle, but with improvements.

The twin-tube chassis was well reinforced with a major cross-bracing plus outriggers and scuttle hoops; the longerons swept up over the rear axle, which was mounted on twin-shackled leaf springs to give lateral location and springing while upper and lower radius arms controlled fore and aft movement and absorbed braking and driving forces. At the front unequal-length wishbones used coil springs on the lower one rather than the earlier car's underslung transverse leaf spring. Houdaille lever-arm dampers were used at both ends, while braking was provided by 14½-in diameter Alfin-type drums within the 16-in wheels; braking was assisted by an engine-driven pump boosting front brake-line pressure. Dimensionally, the wheelbase was 2600 mm (102·4 in) with a mean track of 1346 mm (53 in).

The heart of a Ferrari is always its engine and the 250GT was based on the 250MM Colombo design developed by Lampredi. In its 60 degrees V-12, 73 × 58·8 mm, 2953 cc form, with chain-driven single overhead cam per bank, it wasn't to change throughout the 11 years of the 250GT. Its seven-bearing crankshaft was machined from a solid billet, while the 4·4-in con-rods were forged; silumin — silicon-aluminium alloy — was used for the wet-liner block and the heads; these were sealed by a multiplicity of gaskets — steel, copper and Klingerite. Overhead camshafts were driven by a single triplex chain and operated the valves via roller followers and rockers; these valves sat at a 90 degree included angle in hemispherical chambers, and were constrained by hairpin springs over their 10 mm lift.

Most of the 1954 and 1955 cars used the 250MM Type 112 engines and thus had separate inlet ports per cylinder to develop around 220 bhp, using horizontal front-mounted distributors with plugs inside the vee. However the 1956 cars used the Type 128, an engine that was all new but basically the same apart from the siamesed-port heads, bigger valves, new cams and vertical distributors at the rear; even with three twin-choke 36DCL Webers instead of the 250MM's three four-choke 36IF4C instruments, the output was around the same at 230-240 bhp.

This 128 was developed through into 1958 via the C and D with minor casting differences, a stronger bottom end plus larger inlet valves and tracts to develop up to 260 bhp, depending on cams and compression ratios.

Gradually the Berlinetta lost its resemblance to the 250MM as the bonnet line was lowered and the rear wings became more pronounced. Ferrari had won their first Tour de France in 1956 and were to

The Noblet-'Elde' Ferrari 250GT which finished sixth at Le Mans in 1960, and third in the GT category

Graham Hill leaps out of the Maranello Concessionares GTO during his winning drive in the 1963 TT

do so for the next eight years, so it was not unnatural that the cars which immediately followed that first victory were known as Tour de France models. Best-looking of these was the mid-1957 version, looking almost Aston DB4GT-like with headlamp cowls and horizontal tail fins with a sloping back; the intake was wider and flatter than before moving towards that of the short-wheelbase 250GT. The style continued until mid-1959, although in that year's cars the headlights were moved forward to regain lost light and comply with Italian regulations.

The final move on the old long wheelbase chassis was for Le Mans 1959; the front overhang was shortened, the slope of the rear window (with an air outlet vent attached) decreased, the grille widened, headlights put on extended wings and the Pininfarina wheel had turned full circle, back to the Cisitalia outline, but on to the definitive full circle, that was to rule the GT field from 1960-62. Its purpose was to find more speed for the next generation chassis, and comply with the FIA rules.

After Le Mans 1955, the maximum capacity for prototypes, of which fewer than 100 were built, was 2½-litres for 1956 Le Mans. Then 1957 saw a

reversion to unlimited capacity but with two-seater sports car requirements. However 1958 saw a 3-litre limit which suited Ferrari, who began to press for a GT championship; when Le Mans complied with a GT category for 1959 in advance of the FIA's GT championship of 1960, Ferrari was poised with the new development. In fact, 1959 saw a Tour de France 250GT take third behind the Astons, but one of the new shapes was fourth.

Thus at the Paris Show in October 1959 the new car was unveiled. The Le Mans shape was now on a 2400 mm (94·4 in) wheelbase; the 250GT SWB was born. Under that skin was a new chassis and a further developed engine.

The early cars through to 1960 saw the 128 now in DF form with a new block and heads (128F) and the earlier crankshaft; con-rods now had horizontal joints instead of angled ones, while TR250 heads had outside plugs, bigger valves with coil springs, separate inlet ports and 40DCZ carburettors, to produce around 270 bhp on a 9·5:1 compression ratio in racing trim.

Apart from its wheelbase, the chassis had other changes, although its basic concept of reinforced twin tubes was still evident; the front end was stiffened with more tubes while outriggers were strengthened, and in all the tubular framework was beginning to look more like a Superleggera space frame. Front and rear suspension remained much as before on the same track, but telescopic dampers were now used and Dunlop disc brakes replaced the long-lived drums, still with a power boost to the front, but no vacuum or mechanical pedal servo. The wheels were still 16-in Borrani wires, but 15-in ones were to come in for 1962.

Two versions of the car were produced, Competition and Lusso (luxury). Lusso used steel bodies with a 224 lb overall penalty; the aluminium bodied lightweight weighed in at 1050 kg (2315 lb) at its lightest. Part of that penalty was a cast-iron gearbox casing against the braced silumin one of the racers, while more spartan trim with aluminium interior panels also helped.

Homologation came for the SWB in June 1960, just before Le Mans, while listed options were dry sump lubrication, triple 46DC or six 38DCN Webers, a foretaste of things to come.

The following year saw further engine improvements on the 128E to produce more power for less weight. Bigger valves with revised cams produced the power, lower weight came from the use of elektron castings, while reliability came with a new block with an extra head-bolt per cylinder, single-piece gaskets and heavier rods. In 168 competition form (1961) with the 46 mm carburettors and better breathing the output was around 280 bhp. However with Ferrari finally getting his way for 1962 with the substitution of a GT championship instead of one purely for sports cars, an even quicker car was required to be sure to stay ahead of the Astons and Jaguars for outright victory.

Work on the GTO had started in late 1960 to find more speed and better aerodynamics, the first time that Ferrari had really accepted that engines alone weren't the answer. The SWB ran out at around 155 mph and was getting light at both ends. Much testing ensued on an SWB chassis with a variety of bodies with high speed trips down the autostradas to complement normal Monza or Modena testing. With the dry sump option the engine could be lowered, so a penetrating nose was evolved with the headlights back under perspex cowls, assisted by square 'fog' lights inset beside the now very small intake; when needed, radiator air throughput could be increased by removing one or all of the three trap doors beyond the main intake.

A less sloping tail kept the air better attached so the Kamm tail could produce an advantage in drag reduction, later turned to anti-lift advantage with the duck-tail spoiler, which was more than just a channel to divert fuel overflow from the exhaust pipes. The underside had complete undertrays further to reduce drag.

The trusty engine responded to further development, apart from its dry sump conversion which

The 1964 Ferrari GTO borrowed the LM shape, as the FIA would not homologate the rear-engined car in time

In the 1968 BOAC 500 Rodriguez and Pierpoint drove David Piper's by-then elderly 250LM into fifth place

doubled its oil capacity from 10 to 20 litres. Magnesium was used for sump and rocker covers; further valve and cam work, needle roller followers, bigger ports surmounted by the six 38DCN carburettors forcing the plugs to stay outside the heads, raised the power to all but 300 bhp at 7500 rpm with revs to spare. The crank came from the Testa Rossa sports car, and even the rods were machined from solid billets. Behind this came a brand new five-speed transmission with that delightful open gate at last replacing the four-speed box which was getting a little short on ratios as the power curve became peakier, although tractability was never a problem.

The wheelbase and track remained the same, but the chassis was looking even more 'space frame' with generally smaller tubing. Front and rear suspension used the same design as on the SWB, but the front Konis carried additional springs (as did the rear ones occasionally) while the live rear axle was better located laterally with a Watt linkage. Quick-change calipers were used for still-boosted front brakes and, surprisingly, the hydraulic circuit still only used a single master cylinder.

The 250GTO was announced in February 1962 and gave Ferrari the two GT championships for 1962 and 1963 in its initial form; the GTO had been

accepted as a restyled 250GT, although less than 40 were built over the two years. Perhaps that was why the FIA were cagey over homologating Ferrari's mid-engined 250LM, introduced in 1963.

This led to a hasty revision of the basic GTO, as Ferrari was being threatened by the Cobras. The 1964 GTO used the research that had gone into the LM shape, using less front and rear overhang, and thinner aluminium. The nose was still longer and the tail shorter than on the LM, but the characteristics of the cockpit shape were very much those of the mid-engined car.

The chassis had to stay the same, but extra track was achieved by a combination of hubs and changed offset for wider wheels (now $6\frac{1}{2}$ and $7\frac{1}{2}$ in × 15 in, half an inch more than the previous year) to gain an average 3 in. It was just enough for Ferrari to clinch their third GT championship, but they had to yield GT victory at Le Mans to the Daytona Cobra. The writing was finally on the wall for the 3-litre V-12 which had ruled the roost for the past ten years; brute 4·7-litre force might not have been enough in 1964, but, allied to science in 1965, it gave Ford the victory they sought.

No man-made star can keep shining for ever but Ferrari's two jewels of the early 1960s didn't stay eclipsed in the appeal stakes for very long.

Aston Martin DBR1

The first time I saw DBR1/2 was at Le Mans in 1960, the year after it had won the great long-distance classic with Roy Salvadori and Carroll Shelby at the helm; it had then gone on to clinch the Sports Car Championship for Astons at the Goodwood TT. In 1960, it was in the hands of Major Ian Baillie who, with Jack Fairman, took it to ninth overall; Bailie's three-year ownership was followed by David Ham, Neil Corner and Chris Stewart before current owner Geoffrey Marsh took over the much-raced warrior in 1975 for a complete restoration. Twenty years after the Goodwood success established Aston Martin as the only British winners of the Sports Car Championship, the car was back in better-than-new trim at the Sussex circuit, ready to go.

At Le Mans both DBR1/2 and the dark blue Border Reivers DBR1/3 (Jim Clark and Roy Salvadori, who were to finish third) had impressed as lone and shapely British cars amongst a sea of Ferraris, for there were five TR60s and six 250GTs lined up for the start. The sharp bark of the twin-cam 'sixes' had contrasted with the raspier sound of

the V-12s; always noisier, and frequently spitting flame from the exhaust pipes as they accelerated out of the tight Mulsanne corner, they were music to the ears of a young signaller making his first pilgrimage to the 24-hours. At the end, after long periods of rain, they were more than usually begrimed, dirty dried streaks of dusty rain as testimony to the efficiency of the Frank Feeley shape.

It was hard to believe that it was the same car so pristine and out-of-the-box at Goodwood, but many panels still bear the original markings and very little is new throughout the whole car—almost everything is just reconditioned. I felt I needed a door-mat before stepping on the apparently freshly varnished plywood floor boarding, and a brushing before sitting on a seat, newly reupholstered to the original material specification.

Modern Astons bear the legacy of that cockpit tailor-made for the job; a comfortable seat is sufficiently low off the deck to give a good view across the rounded bonnet, but the low screen was well-enough shaped to deflect air over the head; pedals are nicely spaced with the wood-rimmed

Return to Goodwood with Aston Martin DBR1 No. 2—the most successful of all the DBR1 series

Polished plywood floor and seat re-covered in original specification material

wheel at a comfortable height, but the gear lever was set rather low without a gearbox on which to sit—the David Brown unit is at the rear.

An easy push-start soon had the car under way and on song, giving that stentorian bark under the right ear; the engine pulls from around 2500 rpm but gets going from 3500 rpm towards the day's limit of 6000 rpm. With around 250 bhp in 2070 lb it is quite quick; it lacks the punch of the extra $\frac{3}{4}$-litre of Jaguar unit in a Lister, but, like the Jaguar, it felt as if it would keep going for ever.

Fifth gear is in the forward-right overdrive position, so finger-tip control is required to ensure you get fourth instead of second, but the force required is quite high, which certainly presented occasional problems to the drivers of the day. Having been given suitable reminders of this before setting off, I took great care to be sure I was in the right gear on the approach to a corner, rather than have to make a quick snatch on the way into the apex.

With the engine taken for granted and the gearbox to be treated with respect, it was the chassis that was interesting. The back end seemed firmer in ride than the front, a little bouncy but not enough to upset the grip on bumps; it slides nicely and can be caught with no apparent effort but, put the power down too early, and the inside wheel gets on the threshold of spinning, which seems to have little effect on attitude—just on exit speed.

The front end was less comfortable. Although it turned in nicely with good response to a helm that

feels quite light and sensitive on the approach to a corner, the steering lacks precision once the cornering loads are fed in; it seemed to get heavier, almost masking the feel of changing grip. Under braking and cornering bumps there wasn't just a feel of tyre slip-angles—on top of this was a curious variation in effort required, which might have been gyroscopic in origin; although the front suspension uses twin trailing arms, it shouldn't suffer from precession as the major axes aren't changing angles, unless the arms are bending!

The basic information required was still there once I accepted the weight variation, but it made me feel that oversteer was the safest characteristic as the rear end was most predictable—fortunately it oversteers, although it is quite stable in a straight line.

In fact it would have been very much at home as a Mille Miglia car, blasting along the flat straight of the Italian plains or winding up the Appenine passes; while the brakes were satisfactory the steering might have been hard work on the descents. On the fast flat corners of our airfield circuits, though, it is not at its best—a road car developed into a sports-racer, rather than a sports-racer from scratch. But as it is really a 1956 design we were still in the racing road-car days; that it could win the championship three years later says much for its fundamental rightness.

By 1955 it was clear that the Aston Martin DB3 series, culminating in the purposeful-looking

DB3S, was getting too long in the tooth to remain competitive even in its class. The 1954 Lagonda V-12 with 4½-litres had taken Aston no nearer outright victory, failing within only a few hours at Le Mans in both 1954 and 1955; in the former, the DB3S back-up cars had also failed, but a lone finisher in 1955 had taken second place behind the Hawthorn/Bueb D-type. With victory at Le Mans still his ultimate goal, David Brown ordered a new design to be ready for Le Mans 1956 and the DBR1 was the outcome.

In its time there was little wrong with the DB3S that modernisation couldn't cure—just a little more from each department to make a significant overall improvement. The original Lagonda-type engine had reached the limit of its development in 3-litre form, the chassis needed lightening and its road-holding improved, and a sleeker shape would help on faster circuits.

The DB3S chassis used a ladder-type big tube frame; this carried a de Dion tube at the rear mounted on trailing arms and located laterally by a sliding block. At the front, Porsche-type twin trailing arms were sprung via transverse torsion bars, a system also used at the rear and based on the Auto-Union practice of designer Eberan von Eberhorst. For the DBR1 a completely new and lighter space-frame chassis was created straddling the full width of the car; the front suspension saw

the twin trailing arms retained, but with both transverse torsion bars operating on the lower link and fastened just above the opposite bearing. The upper links are interconnected by a straight anti-roll torsion bar and are integral with Armstrong lever-arm dampers. At the rear, the de Dion tube, two-piece one bolted at its centre, uses radius arms and a transverse Watt linkage. The new chassis saved about 60 lb over that of the DB3S.

The chassis was deliberately stiffened by the engine and a new rear-mounted David Brown gearbox; the DB3S had proved rather short and quick to react, so the two major masses were moved apart and the wheelbase lengthened for the DBR1, to slow its initial response by increasing dumb-bell effect; conversely a spin, once started, takes longer to dissipate.

The DB3S engine had been steadily developed and in its usual 2922 cc form (83 × 90 mm) it had increased its output from 182 bhp on triple 35DCO Weber carburettors to 236 bhp on 40DCO instruments; with the bore up to 84 mm on one engine this became 240 bhp. By this time the aluminium head had valves as large as could be fitted with a 60 degree included angle (1·75 in inlet and 1·55 in exhaust), which squeezed the plug away from the centre, necessitating twin-plug ignition. While the cylinder head was of aluminium, the block was still of cast iron, gradually made heavier by increasing

Twin plug head used on the 3-litre RB6 engine with 95 degree head

cylinder wall thickness to cope with the augmented power.

The new block had to be in aluminium, but, to avoid changing everything at once, it was designed to mate with the existing head, which precluded any variation in bore/stroke ratios or cylinder head fastening. However it was extended below the crankshaft centre line, well reinforced by bracing ribs outside and cross-bolted inside; the counterbalanced crankshaft ran in four main bearings, and cast-iron wet cylinder liners were used. With the 1956 capacity limit for prototypes of $2\frac{1}{2}$-litres (also suited for GP engines) in mind, the stroke was reduced to 76·8 mm, making it oversquare. With Weber 45DCO carburettors and an 8·5:1 compression ratio it gave around 220 bhp, or not much less than the 3-litre DB3S.

The transaxle used a pair of changeable helical gears to drive the first of two transverse shafts, with spur gears taking the drive back to the ZF differential; this set the final drive quite high and the sliding spline drive shafts ran at a pronounced droop. The gearbox had its own dry sump lubrication with interlock valves to squirt oil onto the loaded gears.

This was all clad in the Feeley shape which, on the first car, had more than a hint of DB3 about its grille, and the headlamps were set high in the wing line.

The first car for Brooks/Parnell duly made its debut at Le Mans in 1956, weighing in some 150 lb lighter than the DB3S 3-litre cars. Unfortunately the fuel consumption requirement of around 11 mpg, introduced to limit the fuel load after the 1955 disaster, meant that the thirstier engine had to run weaker than the 3-litre unit, and it suffered from misfiring, but it still survived for 23 hours before retiring with bearing failure when lying seventh.

For 1957 a second car was built and this started with a 3-litre version of the engine using a deeper block and longer con-rods to give 240 bhp on the same 83 × 90 mm, 2922 cc capacity as the old 3-litre. The two cars clocked a 1, 2 at Spa with Brooks ahead of Salvadori in a non-championship race. Nürburgring was a championship event though, and, for 1957, the post-Le Mans 1955 scare had abated somewhat and Appendix C cars could run unlimited by capacity; so the 3-litre Astons started at a disadvantage to the Ferraris and Maseratis but still Brooks/Cunningham-Reid won.

Le Mans was less successful, for either of the two DBR1s or the new DBR2. This looked similar to the DBR1 but used the earlier backbone-type Lagonda V-12 chassis with a 3-in longer wheelbase and $1\frac{1}{2}$-in greater track; its engine was the 3·7-litre DB4 with the Lagonda's DB five-speed gearbox mated to it, while the suspension followed DBR1 design. However Brooks had one of the DBR1s up to second place for some time before gearbox trouble intervened and eventually led to his overturning into the sand, while the other had an oil pipe failure; the DBR2 had its own gearbox trouble.

By now the new head was ready, with fiercer camshafts driven by a train of gears instead of chains, and the valve angle was widened to 95 degrees allowing 2-in inlet and 1·6-in exhaust valves; power was up to 250 bhp at 6000 rpm on a 9·25:1 compression ratio, but the peak torque of an admittedly flat curve was at 5500 rpm, placing a premium on gearchanging on an awkward and then fragile box.

Brooks won again at Spa and the two cars then came fourth and sixth at the International Trophy behind the two DBR2s, first and third, bracketing Scott-Brown's Lister-Jaguar.

At one stage the DBR2s were likely contenders for the 1958 championship, but that was reduced to 3-litres again. However work continued on the DBR2s in 1958 National races with capacity up to 3·9-litres; finally they were shipped out to America at the end of 1958 with 4·2-litres and 315 bhp. As a result of the good performance of the DB4 engine, a

DBR3 was built using a short-stroke version for 3-litres, while the DBR1 chassis was adapted to take wishbone front suspension, but its sole race in 1958 saw the engine seize and the car was converted back to DBR1/4.

However the start of the 1958 season saw the two original DBR1s go to Sebring, but transmission failure sidelined the Moss car near half-distance, not before the car had showed a clean pair of heels to the might of Maranello, while the other suffered a chassis failure. Moss then took the new DBR1/3 to the Targa Florio, but was again put out by transmission failure, despite or as a result of shattering his own Mercedes 300SLR lap record.

Three cars at the Nürburgring produced one victor (Moss with only a little help from Brabham), one crash and another transmission failure. At Le Mans, Moss led for two hours before a rod broke, Lewis-Evans lost it on the fast Dunlop curve during the rain, but Brooks/Trintignant stayed in the top five until retiring in the 15th hour in third place with ... transmission failure. The Whiteheads salvaged second in their DB3S.

With Ferrari having won the championship, a Ferrari-less TT presented an easy 1, 2, 3 for the Astons, a good finish after a disappointing season that they might have won had less development time been expended on the DBR2s. Wider input spur gears before this event had finally cured the problems on DBR1 transmissions.

That winter saw further engine development with a seven-bearing block to increase rigidity if not power with 50DCO Weber carburettors, but they compensated for friction losses.

David Brown still wanted to win Le Mans above all, but sent a single car to Sebring and met with failure. The same car, DBR1/1, went solo to the Nürburgring with 254 bhp, as a result of bigger valves and the lower friction four-bearing block; here Moss drove one of his great races, wresting back the lead after Fairman had been forced off in the rain and then lifted the car out of a ditch. It was the third Aston victory in a row at the 'Ring and the second for DBR1/1.

Le Mans 1959 saw David Brown's ambition finally achieved and heightened by a 1, 2 after Moss' early pace had broken the back of the Ferrari onslaught; Salvadori/Shelby first led in the seventh hour, were overhauled by the Gendebien//Hill Ferrari until that overheated in the 20th hour, and then led to the finish.

With no Venezuelan race, the TT became crucial for Ferrari, Porsche and Aston all in with a chance. Moss/Salvadori set the pace from the front, making good use of nitrogen-operated on-car jacks, and were leading at 2½ hours when Salvadori pitted; the Aston's characteristic back-fire after switching off set light to spilled fuel, and car and pit went up in flames. Moss then took over the Fairman/Shelby car, hauled in all ahead and took the flag for TT and championship. It was the crowning moment for David Brown—Le Mans and the Manufacturer's Sports Car Championship in one year; so Aston Martins retired from sports car racing, albeit temporarily, and the DBR1 had earned itself a coveted place in motor racing history, which was the more remarkable as it was by then a 3-year-old design.

The Le Mans-winning Aston in 1959, with Salvadori driving the travel-stained DBR1

Lister–Jaguar

The harsh bark of 3·8-litres of tuned Jaguar echoed off the grassy bank as the revs rose and fell before the off; with 4000 rpm on the clock, the single-plate competition clutch bit home, the 6·50L × 15-in Dunlop racers left straight and parallel black streaks on the tarmac, the long shapely nose lifted under power and the Lister was off like a rocket; 30 mph came and went in 2 sec, 60 mph took a mere 4·8 sec, 100 mph in 10·5 sec, 1100 mph and the quarter-mile post went together in 12·8 sec, and in 20 sec — or less time than you have taken to read this far — we were doing 130 mph with the kilometre covered in 23·6 sec.

'We' were Lister–Jaguar BHL 133, Costin-bodied and formerly Chevrolet powered, plus an *Autocar* contribution of John Miles and fifth wheel test equipment, establishing just how well my own car accelerated on the Motor Industry Research Association test track. With 315 bhp in 1900 lb (nearer 2300 lb as tested with two up and test kit) it has a very useful power/weight ratio and the figures were impressive for a 20-year-old car.

What was also impressive was the way the car put its power down through what are relatively skinny tyres in today's high performance terms. It is always good at that, even in the wet.

By then I had had a season with BHL 133, using a modified 3·8-litre wet-sump engine which had started life in a road-going Mk. IX Jaguar, but prepared by Forward Engineering to give its

315 bhp at 6000 rpm; the particularly harsh bark was a function of a pair of unsilenced three-into-one tuned-length exhaust pipes, responsible for an extra 15 bhp against the standard Jaguar cast-iron enamelled manifolds.

However the engine is still very torquey; at its best beyond 3500 rpm it can still potter around the paddock at 1000 rpm without oiling plugs, and can maintain this astonishingly docile behaviour for a season's racing with no adjustment.

The season before I had driven the ex-Peter Mould YOB 575 (or BHL 120), a 1958 car with the 'knobbly' body; that had a wide-angle D-type dry sump engine with slightly less power but with that famed wide-angle torque. With a 4·1 final drive (against my 3·77) and 16-in wheels, it was faster than my own car, but it was some time before I could get it to handle as well and achieve faster lap times.

Sitting in YOB I was very conscious of the screen, set behind the bulging bonnet, and the high tail with its little headrest; its seat was a cushion on the floor matching a padded back rest poppered to the shaped rear bulkhead; I sat low and almost looked through the screen just over a large wood-rimmed wheel; behind it were the usual instruments plus speedometer and rev counter each side of the centre line.

In my own car I sit higher on a seat and find it much easier to place despite the more bulbous

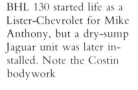
BHL 130 started life as a Lister-Chevrolet for Mike Anthony, but a dry-sump Jaguar unit was later installed. Note the Costin bodywork

In behaviour the two cars are very similar. Into a corner you get a slightly indirect understeer which is exaggerated in the wet; but put the power down and the tail comes round, not in a great slide but merely a change of direction unless the power is deliberately excessive — the cars are very throttle responsive and you can balance them according to your own driving style by playing with spring rates.

The engine is set well back in the chassis with the gearbox virtually amidships, so the weight distribution is virtually 50/50, but the rearward mass is well back — de Dion tube, final drive and fuel tank — so there is a certain amount of inertia behind; add that to the hub-height rear roll centre and it isn't easy to catch a tail slide once it starts unless you are very quick and anticipate it, or unless you ease the throttle in which case it isn't easy to catch cleanly; if it starts to spin when you are off the throttle, it'll just keep on. The steering is, in fact, quite low geared with parallel steering arms and an inverted lhd Minor rack so initial response is slow although feel is good; bodywork; my steering wheel is smaller and I have fewer instruments, just oil pressure and water temperature with a rev counter and an ammeter on the left.

On a D-type gearbox the lever sits behind the casing on its own pivot, which is rather far back for comfort; YOB has a forward cranked lever to get the hand nearer the steering wheel; on my car, the close ratio road-going Moss box has a similar system, but I have since changed this to a conventional top which sits the lever direct in the selectors and is much more convenient.

the lock is poor and worse with a Costin body with its cowled wheels unless you bell out the arches. All of which makes them quite hard to drive quickly, but always a challenge.

Brakes are by Girling with CR/BR front/rear aluminium calipers; these spread visibly under pedal pressure and it is essential to keep the pads faced flat or you get a spongy pedal. They need a lot of cooling air too, particularly for the inboard rear discs shrouded under the bodywork — and fuel tank too if you still have a long-distance capacity — but when they are set up properly they work very well, pulling the nose down sharply when you hit the pedal.

In lap times Listers are capable of averaging over 100 mph around the Silverstone GP circuit with its Woodcote chicane, but I'm still 0·3 mph under. In ultimate terms the maximum is probably over 160 mph but the fastest I have seen in mine on the 3·77 axle is 145 mph at 6500 rpm; in YOB at Le Mans with a 2·88 axle and 15-in wheels we could only pull 5400 rpm or just under 160 mph, by which speed the wind was getting under the bonnet and lifting the body. But both are impressively stable when running quickly.

Of the two, I prefer the 'knobbly' shape, but like my own car more; although it has no great history it was the last of the normal-framed Listers, the last of the line that started as Mr Brian's special for Archie Scott-Brown.

The big Listers were one enthusiast's answer to the finally dated Jaguar D-type which, by 1958, had

BHL 105, the Equipe Nationale Belge car, at Le Mans in 1958, where it was driven by Rouselle and Dubois. It lost oil pressure in the fourth hour

Following pages: the author in the knobbly-bodied Lister-Jaguar YOB 575 at Brands Hatch

given four years sound service to the Coventry factory, placing them in the top three of the Sports Car Championship from 1953-7, ably assisted by Ecurie Ecosse. Good though it was, the D-type had become too heavy and unsophisticated to keep up with the lightweight Italian cars on any track but Le Mans, where aerodynamics and reliability take over; with the imposition of a 3-litre limit for 1958, the D-type was at an even greater disadvantage although the Scottish team continued to campaign them throughout 1958.

The enthusiast who wanted to keep the British and Jaguar flag flying, was Brian Lister, grandson of the founder of George Lister and Sons, a respected Cambridge engineering firm. The first Lister, MER 303, saw the light of day in 1954 powered by MG TD and was the product of Brian Lister (Light Engineering) Cambridge Ltd; its driver on its Oulton Park debut was to be Archie Scott-Brown, although Jack Sears finally drove the car first as Scott-Brown's unformed hand initially precluded him from racing outside club events.

More power had to come and the next car, MVE 303, was powered by Bristol, making its debut at the British GP meeting in 1954 where Scott-Brown ran away with the 2-litre class and finished fifth overall, the first of many successes through to 1955 for the green cars with the yellow stripe. Production started in 1955 with Lister-Bristols on general sale and some 20 were to be built. The following year saw the 'works' run with 2-litre Maserati power in MER 303, in an attempt to get even nearer the front runners, but the engine was for ever consuming its pistons and valve gear, and 1956 was a poor year.

Meanwhile privateer Norman Hillwood had a strengthened Lister–Bristol chassis prepared and inserted a wet-sump 3·4-litre C-type engine and gearbox; LMK 673 was thus the first Lister–Jaguar. However, Brian Lister was also working on the same theory and the 1957 works entry was to be the rebuilt MVE 303, with a dry-sump 3·4-litre D-type and gearbox with a bigger Salisbury axle.

Throughout Lister production the basic chassis design was to remain the same. The basic frame was twin 3-in diameter tubes splayed around the cockpit and braced by three similar cross members. At the front, box sections sprouted vertically to carry upper and lower wishbones and rack and pinion steering; the wishbones were tubular and fabricated of equal length with coil spring/damper units mounted between them; the kingpost was Lister built on the lines of the MG TD; an anti-roll bar was to follow. At the rear, a de Dion tube ran round the back of the final drive unit and was located laterally by a bolt through its centre holding a bronze block, which moved in guides attached to the chassis behind the diff. Fore and aft location was via upper and lower radius arms each side trailing from a pillar sprouting from the chassis; coil and damper units joined the de Dion tube to the chassis.

Although the design was fundamentally an improvement over the Jaguar D-type, being lighter and with a better rear suspension, it wasn't perfect. A ground level front roll-centre is low on roll

resistance and the wheels change camber with body roll; at the rear a hub-height roll centre is conversely higher than ideal, taking too much of the weight transfer, so that it is difficult to sort out ideal spring rates and you need a strong front anti-roll bar to balance it. With only single deck chassis rails the frame wasn't overstrong when it came to bigger engines, although some stiffness is conferred by a stressed undertray up to the sills. But, considering that it was basically a 1953 design it showed sound thinking, and the whole was laid out to get a near 50/50 weight distribution with the engine mounted well back, the battery amidships and fuel and oil tanks in the tail.

With the recreated MVE 303, Scott-Brown had an incredible 1957 season winning 12 out of 14 races, the only track defeat being at the hands of Salvadori's 3·7-litre Aston DBR2 in mid-season, by which time the Lister was using a 3·8-litre engine.

Success for MVE continued in New Zealand with two victories, one against single-seaters, two failures (suspension and diff) and a sixth. Meanwhile the Lister reputation had spread and the Cambridge factory embarked on quantity production of the big Lister to the tune of some 38 or so chassis over the next two years. Changes to the MVE specification included a new chassis with wheelbase up from 7 ft 5 in to 7 ft 6¾ in and 1½ in on the track at each end, now 4 ft 4 in and 4 ft 5½ in; Girling 12-in discs with quick-change CR/BR calipers replaced the previous 11-in front, 10-in rear set up.

Appendix C regulations already specified such dimensions as 13 cm minimum ground clearance, 12 m maximum turning circle, 20 cm vertical height for the screen (later increased to 25 cm), minimum interior width of 120 cm across the steering wheel over a depth of 25 cm, equal comfort front seats with minimum leg dimensions for pedal to seat back, plus cushion to floor of 110 cm, door size of 50 × 30 cm, driver's foot width of 25 cm, and so on. So the new car was built around these dimensions; in fact the body was the same, 1½ in wider than MVE, as was the track but, at 13 ft 6 in it was 6 in longer. Lister cleverly masked the effect of the high screen by placing it behind a bonnet bulge for the engine and used a near screen-top tail height to reattach the air flow. Forward, the bonnet line hugged the engine down to a remote radiator and the large front wheel bulges gave the name 'knobbly' to the body style.

For International racing the engine limit was set at 3 litres although UK and US national races continued to run to *Formule Libre*, so Listers left the factory with 3, 3·4 or 3·8-litre Jaguar engines, or just a space for Americans who wanted to fit small-block Chevrolet engines and gearboxes; these started life as 4·6-litre V-8s, but the American penchant for 'boring and stroking' soon had them up to 5·7 litres with rather more reliability than they originally showed.

Reducing Jaguar's engine to 3 litres sounds a recipe for a good unstressed unit, but the engine chosen was the lighter 2·4 with a stroke of 76·5 mm against 106 mm and a consequent 1⅝ in off the top of the block; the bore was the same as in the 3·4 at

83 mm. Jaguar squeezed in a 92 mm crankshaft and the resultant 254 bhp at 6300 rpm was more than the 3·4 had produced; however the greater revs overstressed the valvegear in longer races and the engines lacked the famed D-type reliability.

For Listers, the 1958 International season started at Sebring when Briggs Cunningham had the first two production 'big Listers' BHL 101 and 102; 106 joined them later for a Chevrolet engine. Scott-Brown was teamed with Walt Hansgen in a promising pairing, but the car was shunted up the tail by Gendebien's Ferrari before the race was five laps old. Crawford in the other car suffered the valve trouble that afflicted all Jaguar engines that day.

But at home things were better and Scott-Brown in VPP 9, which had started life as Lister–Bristol BHL 3, was near invincible although the 3·7-litre DBR2s did get ahead on occasions. The third car had gone to privateer Peter Whitehead, later to be used so successfully by John Bekaert; however the fourth went to Ecurie Ecosse for Masten Gregory to drive. Having beaten Gregory at Aintree, Scott-Brown was beaten by him at the BRDC Silverstone, Gregory establishing the first official 100 mph sports-car lap, although Scott-Brown had been faster in practice at 1 min 43 sec, 102·3 mph.

Thus when these two went to Spa a fortnight later to take part in a Libre event there was rivalry in the air; against them were ranged other Listers—the Whitehead car, Rouselle (Equipe National Belge) in BHL 105, and Halford in HCH 736, a little Lister that had grown from BHL 5—plus the Astons and some D-types.

Gregory was fastest in practice from Scott-Brown and, when the race was under way it was these two taking turns at leading on a damp track when Scott-Brown entered Club House corner, freshly wetted after a local shower; the little wizard from Cambridge lost control, crashing into a field in flames to die shortly afterwards. That Gregory went on to win Lister's only Continental victory mattered little—Lister's leading light had gone.

Brian Lister nearly gave up racing there and then, but was persuaded against it and Ivor Bueb joined the team. MVE 303 had been recreated as a big Lister and another VPP 9 was built; Moss drove the

former at the British GP meeting and Hansgen the latter—Moss won. Bueb drove both cars during the rest of the season with reasonable success.

At the end of 1958, International success had eluded the Listers but they were very quick with the 3·8-litre at home; in America, Hansgen was winning more often than not. By the end of the year some 20 cars had been built of which probably five Jaguar and seven Chevrolet-powered cars had gone to America.

Le Mans was still something of a goal, though, and that year had only seen privateers competing— the Belgian car which didn't finish and HCH 736 with Halford/Naylor just making it into 15th position. For 1959 Brian Lister signed up Frank Costin to design a new body on a virtually identical chassis with marginally longer rear radius rods and Dunlop brakes to match the wheels and tyres.

Costin's body followed his earlier themes of long tapering bonnet, elliptical cross section, faired in wheels and compound-curved front and side screens blending into a high tail—at 14 ft 4¾ in and 5 ft 7 in it was 10¾ in longer and 4½ in wider. It was shapely but proved to be little faster.

The first outing saw Moss/Bueb in a Cunningham entry leading at Sebring but they were disqualified for receiving outside assistance when they ran out of fuel. Le Mans saw another attempt with Bueb/Halford and Hansgen/Blond, but neither lasted and both were behind the Ecosse Tojeiro-Jaguar and D-type when the engines gave up.

When Ivor Bueb was killed—not in a Lister— Brian Lister withdrew from racing and the works entry for the final International, the TT, was taken over by Sieff/Blond; their car lost water and retired. That also marked the end of Lister production, although Costin's space-frame chassis development was to appear on just one car.

By then mid-engined cars were taking over and new designs were needed. To continue would be expensive and the basic purpose of publicity for the company had been achieved; Brian Lister returned to the engineering side of the business, where he is still; his cars are still on the tracks and he takes pride in their achievements—there can only have been about five years between the last of the Listers in club racing and their rebirth in historic events.

At Sebring in 1959 Stirling Moss demonstrated the promise of the Costin-bodied Listers, although he was disqualified for receiving outside assistance

Lotus 15

Colin Chapman's reputation was founded on lightweight efficiency, whether on road or track, but small though his cars were they didn't lack performance; power/weight ratio and an excess of grip over weight soon had them much further up the grids than mere engine size would suggest. As a former club-racer, Chapman designed his early sports-racers for the UK tracks, but success there bred greater ambitions and engine-size options grew. It was logical to choose the one of many similar-looking designs that was the most competitive front-runner—the Lotus 15, developed through the 8, 9, 10 and 11 with a bit of help from the first of the single-seaters, the F2 12.

Mike Weatherill, who used to race the 7, 11 and Elite in their day, owned a 15 and I joined him in a test day at Goodwood which, with its air of sad neglect, is still a nice circuit to drive round and with its dips and adverse cambers is much more of a challenge than, say, Silverstone.

The 15 came with a choice of Climax engines from 1½ to 2½ litres. While awaiting the installation of a 2-litre, this one was fitted with the 1½-litre twin-cam FPF with a preservative rev limit of 6000 rpm, against the originally quoted 142 bhp at 7200 rpm. In common with the production Series 2 and 3, a normal four-speed gearbox is fitted, rather than the Chapman integral gearbox/final drive of the early 15s.

There is actually a door, which opens enough for one to put a gentle foot on to a convenient chassis tube on the inside of the sill, and then lower away into the narrow confines of the seating area.

Mike Weatherill is somewhat bigger and drove without a seat; I had to sit on and be pressed forward by suitable sorbo padding. Like a lot of 'fours' in racing vehicles, the engine isn't particularly smooth

at rest, but as you move off with a bit of revs and a bit of load, it smooths out and pulls strongly from the middle range and would be quite happy beyond 6000 rpm.

Despite sorbo the driving position was ideal; not much room for feet or even for twirling elbows, but then a Lotus never has required much twirling and the lock is fairly limited by the bodywork. You sit back and steer at arm's length with the gear lever within a handspan of the left hand. With a slight kick-up on the driver's side of the perspex screen, 5 ft 8 in can look over the top without getting windswept; it was only in the left-handed St. Mary's dip that I found I had to look through it. The mirror sits on top of the screen with stays down to the scuttle top and gives a view that can be described as adequate, without being at all comprehensive.

With under 1100 lb and around 120 bhp to play with—up to 6000 rpm—the acceleration is brisk without being startling; it just moves up rapidly to 100 mph (5300 rpm) and beyond without any obvious effort, so good are the aerodynamics. The bonnet starts to flap a bit beyond 90 mph. The necessary silencer for Goodwood made it very quiet, too, at the expense of a rather warm right thigh—the system runs inside the sill to its outlet just in front of the rear wheel. The gearbox is the ZF unit that was available on Elites at the time and is very slick in its short travel movement, with ratios that suit the car well.

It is difficult to put across the level of roadholding on any car without a g-meter, but in their heyday those Lotus sports cars were always beating cars of considerably greater capacity, so the roadholding was obviously better than most. Even now, it still feels very good even on appropriately narrow tyres—5·00L × 15-in front and 5·50L × 15-in rear,

The sleek lines of the Lotus 15 are very evident in this shot

Instant servicing accessibility on the Lotus 15, here with a 1·5-litre FPF Climax engine

Dunlop, of course. There is a complete absence of apparent roll and the car just responds to the steering wheel; on the overrun and under braking the rear suspension design countersteers, which would lead to oversteer under power, but the overall system is set up to understeer under power for slower corners, which the aerodynamics adjust to slight oversteer on faster corners. Apart from spring rates and damper settings there isn't a lot of adjustment available as roll bars require replacement. In fact on slow corners there is enough power surplus to get through the understeer—round Woodcote for instance and out of the chicane.

Light cars don't make a lot of effort to stop with 9½-in diameter discs all round, and the 15 seems to go almost impossibly deep into corners before the slightly soft pedal anchors the car firmly down. It is a very reassuring car to drive in all ways and as long as you have enough engine spares—FPFs are getting rare—it is easy to maintain and keep going; Herald uprights, ZF box (or an MGA equivalent) and BMC A series differential are easier to find than many equivalents on other makes. I enjoyed it very much and it seemed an eminently suitable car in which to go historic racing, although doubtless one would soon start wanting the extra power of the 2 or 2¼ litre.

It is logical to start the story of the 15 with the 8, which was the first of the aerodynamically shaped Lotus sports racers. Peter Gammon's MG-engined Mk. 6 was doing well in 1953 and Chapman wanted to take on the 1500 cc 'establishment', which at that time meant Cooper, Tojeiro, Connaught and, of course, Porsche. Lotus then meant Colin Chapman and Mike Costin, so Frank Costin was brought in to design the bodywork of the new car while

Chapman evolved a chassis better than that of the 6. It was still a lightweight space frame and retained the divided or swing-axle front suspension, but used a de Dion at the rear with inboard drums and it was sprung by a single transverse helical spring above. Brakes were drums all round with air ducting. The body was certainly a departure from that of the usual sports car and was effectively Frank Costin's first essay into automobile aerodynamics. Thus it had a long, penetrating nose, coming almost to a point at hub-height with the extension of the full-length undertray, while the tail extended back and up, into pronounced fins to give the course stability required in the aircraft world; the rear wheels were faired in with spats—removed or cut back on some cars—while the front wheel arches followed the shape of the wheel in front but were cut vertically behind close to the wheel. The exhaust system was contained in the sills and exited in front of the rear wheel. The popular choice of engine was the uprated TC of 1467 cc, but the Climax 1100 was also fitted and John Coombs used a 1½-litre Connaught engine, which was eventually the fastest 8. The final drive incidentally was cooled by a prop-shaft-driven pump and oil from the engine.

For 1955 some drivers were wanting to install ever larger engines in their 8s, notably Mike Anthony who wanted to put a Bristol engine in. Enlarging the engine compartment and putting a bulge in the bonnet top to clear even a lowered Bristol was all that was outwardly necessary, but underneath, disc brakes were added, while the de Dion was located on the usual radius arm and transverse rod with conventional coil/damper units. This was the Lotus 10.

Meanwhile, Chapman had been working on a version of the 8 for smaller engines, notably the

1100 FWA Climax and perhaps the 1500 FWB version. The idea was to use as many common parts as possible in the 9 in its competition form and the 10, hence the revised de Dion location with special cast Elektron hub-carriers. Lighter than the 8, the 9 used the same wheelbase, but was 2 ft shorter overall, losing a little in the nose, but rather more behind, although taller fins kept the course stability the same; this had been as a result of wool-tuft tests with Frank Costin strapped to the bonnet for some runs! The rear of the front wheel arch was less suddenly chopped into the body with a more gradual escape path for the air around the wheels.

The 9 came in Club form with normal drum brakes and a Ford 10 rear axle, using the de Dion locating linkage; in its Le Mans competition form, the drums were steel-lined Elektron castings of, initially, 9-in diameter, rising to 11 in. At the front the divided axle was retained but the roll centre was lowered by dropping the pivot point. Chapman's fears of gyroscopic reaction at high speeds had not been realised and it was reasonable to continue with the swing axle.

The Le Mans came after Chapman and Ron Flockhart had taken a 9 to Le Mans; Chapman had been racing with the $1\frac{1}{2}$-litre MG engine, but took an 1100 Climax car to Le Mans. This had heavier gauge panelling and discs to help negotiate Mulsanne. After one hour the Lotus was leading the 1100 class just ahead of the Duntov/Veuillet Porsche which eventually finished 13th, but that and another 356 were soon ahead and the Lotus was fighting it out with the Wadsworth/Brown Cooper-Climax. Unfortunately the car was disqualified after 11 hours, when Chapman reversed out of a sandbank at Arnage without being ushered by a marshal; at this point they were 27th overall and ahead of the Cooper, which went on to take 21st place and third in the 1100 class.

With the 9 and 10 in various forms running concurrently in 1955, Chapman decided to produce just one model for 1956 and that was the 11. This was to be available in three forms under the same skin; the 11 retained the same scuttle height as that of the 9 but the bonnet dropped away more quickly, which accentuated the wheel humps. At both ends the wheels were hidden to just above hub height. The rear finning had all but gone, although high speed competition cars could have a headrest fairing to retain the sidewind stability. It was 6 in shorter than the 9 and the new frame gave a wheelbase $2\frac{1}{2}$ in shorter; like the 9, it was designed to take the Climax engine in FWA and FWB forms, giving 83 or 100 bhp. All models retained the divided axle, but the Le Mans had de Dion rear suspension, still with upper and lower radius arms, but with an inclined arm on the right-hand side to make up an A-bracket with the lower radius arm and provide lateral location. Disc brakes were fitted all round ($9\frac{1}{2}$ in diameter) and the car scaled just under 900 lb. The height to the scuttle top was just 2 ft 3 in, while even to the top of the fin it was only 3 ft 1 in.

The Club model came with a BMC axle, using the same location as the de Dion version, drum

brakes all round and the 1100 Climax. Finally the Sports model was tailored for the Ford 1172 cc engine. The 1956 return to Le Mans saw three cars built specially, with slightly wider cockpit areas and full-width screens for the regulations—there were two 1100s and one 1500. Cliff Allison's 1100 was put out by a dog on the Mulsanne straight at dawn, then Chapman's 1500 broke a big-end bolt with 4 hours to go when it was lying 18th, although it had been as high as 11th. However the remaining Bicknell/Jopp 1100 kept going until the end and finished an astounding seventh, winning the 1100 class from the Hugus/Bentley Cooper, eighth.

Meanwhile, Chapman had been working on the first single-seater Lotus, the 12 for the 1500 F2, with the new dohc FPF 'four' giving 142 bhp at 7200 rpm. This used a space frame chassis, but dispensed with the divided axle front suspension in favour of wishbones in which the forward link of the upper wishbone formed an arm of the anti-roll bar. At the rear, the original design had included a de Dion tube with single radius arms, a central link and a semi trailing Panhard rod, but this was dispensed with in favour of a design which allowed camber change with lessening fuel loads and the Chapman strut was born; this used a MacPherson strut arrangement with an aluminium hub carrier, a shrunk-in coil/spring damper strut, with the lateral location on the drive shaft and an inclined radius arm.

The gearbox arrangement used a Lotus design integral with the final drive. Using a low transmission line with a two-piece prop shaft the gearbox was a simple two-shaft unit with five pairs of gears in constant mesh, engaged by dogs and controlled by a lever, which zig-zagged forwards for higher gears and back for downchanges—an ingenious device which required a little early sorting in its lubrication but otherwise worked fairly well for that torque application. The 12 marked the first appearance of the wobbly-web bolt-on magnesium alloy wheels, too.

For 1957, the 11 continued, but in Series 2 form for the two Le Mans models—the Le Mans 85 and Le Mans 150 the latter using the FPF unit. The Series 2 changes were to use the wishbone front suspension from the 12 and enlarge the de Dion tube to take bigger bearings, while the bodywork was flared out to take the wider wheels; some were using wobbly-webs instead of the old knock-on spoked variety.

Le Mans 1957 saw five 11s entered with one on the reserve list—a 1500 FPF, three 1100s and a 750 with only the latter, which would probably not need a tyre change, on the bolt-on wheels. Unfortunately, the FPF dropped a valve in practice and that was that, so four cars started and four cars finished, with the MacKay Fraser/Chamberlain car finishing ninth overall and winning the 1100 class, and the Allison/Hall 750 winning its class and the Index of Performance in 14th place overall, averaging 90 mph, 10 mph faster than the previous winning DB Panhard's speed.

With the 1500 breaking the class record in practice, Chapman's thoughts for 1958 were turning towards outright victory when he conceived the 15 to take the FPF in 2 and 2·2-litre forms. This was really the successor to the 10 for bigger engines, but embodied all that had been learnt in the Series 2 11s, with the addition of the 12's strut rear suspension. The radius arm was mounted further out than with the single-seater and was a dog-legged trailing arm. For the gearbox, the Lotus 12 unit was used with the gear selection changed to the 16's positive stop motor-cycle system, back for down-changes and forward for upwards. As a successor to the 10 the 15 used the 88-in wheelbase—3 in up on the 11 and 3 in longer, too. The engine was canted over 60 degrees to the right with special long curved manifolds for the Webers or twin-choke SUs, which the 12s had been using; this allowed the car to be even lower than the 11 at 2 ft to the top of the scuttle. The fins were similar to those of the 11, while the head-fairing became standard, since it housed the vertical spare wheel; it was a very slippery shape which had a theoretical maximum of 205 mph on the 2·2-litre FPF. To cater for the Appendix C rules, the cockpit was larger than an 11's and the screen was a full-width item carefully profiled. They were very fast first time out at the British Empire Trophy in 1958, with Hill taking the lap record at Oulton Park, which Moss had to equal in the DBR2 Aston to stay in front of Allison in the final.

Le Mans 1958 saw six specially prepared Lotus, four works cars and two privateers. The canted engine with the long curving inlets had proved to lose power so the 2-litre car had the FPF canted 17 degrees to the left, like the 12. Hill and Allison were to drive the 2-litre 15 with an eye to possible outright victory, Chamberlain/Lovely had the 1·5-litre, Ireland and Michael Taylor the 1100 cc 11, and Stacey/Dickson a 750 cc 11, with the FWM single-cam engine up to 750, rather than the modified FWA of the previous year. Another FWM 11 and an 1100 cc 11 were private entries.

The 750 cc cars saved transmission losses with live axles and were using drum brakes and magnesium wheels, while the 15s had knock-ons. Unfortunately it was a disastrous year for Lotus; the 2-litre had gone impressively fast in practice, but blew a gasket after three laps, the 1·5-litre had ignition trouble and was finally shunted. One 1100 wasn't allowed to restart after spinning on the Mulsanne straight, but the other kept going and had been up to 12th place, before the distributor failed after 19 hours, when it was the sole 1100 running; one 750 was involved in a White House shunt while the Stacey/Dickson 750 was the sole surviving Lotus in 20th position and well behind the other 750s.

In mid-1958 a Series 2 version of the 15 was announced as an export version with easier servicing; consequently it used a conventional BMC B-series box with a BMC A-series final drive in a Lotus casing. One of the 15's more memorable performances in 1958 was at the British GP where Salvadori in Coombs' 2-litre came second to Moss' Lister–Jaguar to win the 2-litre class, while Allison was third winning the 1500 class and Stacey fifth to win the 1100 class in his 11.

The year 1959 saw the arrival of the 11's

replacement for small capacity engines and that was the 17, shorter, narrower and even lower than the 11; it followed on from the 16 in using some glass-fibre panels. The rear suspension used the Chapman strut system and the front suspension, too, used a strut, although this was changed to wishbones later. It was available with the FWM or FWE engines. The 15 continued as the Series 3 with a stiffer chassis, the upper wishbone was reversed to allow a bigger radiator—the anti-roll bar was now behind hub-centre line—and the engine was now angled like the Le Mans 2-litre at 17 degrees to the left; the transmission followed the Series 2 in having a separate gearbox and final drive.

For Le Mans outright victory was again the goal and a 2½-litre FPF was entered for Hill and Derek Jolly while Ireland/Stacey were to have a 2-litre. A pair of 17s had FWM engines with an eye on the Index of Performance. In fact only one 15 arrived with a 2-litre engine, using a version of the 16 gearbox, which now lay on its side in the single-seater but was vertical in the 15. The 2-litre unit was replaced by a 2½-litre before the race and the car, driven by Hill/Jolly was seventh at the end of the first hour but lost time with a prop-shaft bearing failure, then broke a wishbone and finally dropped a rod. The two 17s suffered distributor trouble which caused over-heating, and it was left to the Elites to maintain the Lotus name, with Lumsden/Riley finishing eighth and Clark/Whitmore 10th.

At the Brands F2 meeting Hill won in the 2½-litre 15 from David Piper's 2-litre. The TT saw 15s out with 2-litre engines; Hill's car had ignition trouble and Piper's crashed when a tyre failed.

It is probably fair to say that at that time, the 15 suffered from lack of development while the accent was on Grand Prix racing. At the end of 1959 the mid-engined era had arrived and the 18 was Lotus' ubiquitous single-seater, which led to the Monte Carlo 19 and the 15 was instantly obsolete.

Le Mans pit stop in 1957, with Cliff Allison leaping into the class-winning Lotus 11, with a 750 cc FWM engine

Following pages: (left) Lotus were always designed for small people; even 5 ft 8 in is looking well over the top of the screen, but the lip diverts the air effectively. *(right)* In conditions like these the Lola really scores over more powerful rivals; here Belgian Willie Widar proves the point with Minilite wheels looking reasonably period

Lola Mk.I

I'd often wondered why a little Lola Mk.I with a 1098 cc Climax engine proved capable of beating some of the Lister–Jaguars around the 1959-61 period—not only on the tight circuits but on faster ones as well. After all, even 90 bhp in 900 lb shouldn't be enough to keep up with 265 bhp in 2020 lb, and the driver of the bigger car should be able to make it wide enough on the corners.

My chance to see some of the reasons came with a test drive in BR 31, then owned by Mike Ostroumoff; prior to that it had started life as a 1962 car for Bluebelle Gibbs who had driven it for many years; ex-Lister driver David Beckett then used it for early historic races and achieved much the same effect that history itself had shown. Bill James ran it briefly, then Ostroumoff, and it has since gone to Germany to Hubertus Donhoff. As a 1962 car it had started with disc brakes and taken the post-1960 options used on some with a 1216 cc Climax engine and 13-in wheels.

It is certainly a compact little car which you drop down into and almost lie within, as long as you are of average height. Pedals, wheel and gear lever were all easy to operate from a comfortable position; the least comfortable aspect was a hot left leg from gearbox and engine heat—no bonnet outlet louvres—but it wasn't unpleasant on a cold day. With a canted engine there is only a small bulge in a low bonnet line, and that is out of sight on the left, so the view forward is very good and it is easy to place the car accurately.

With twin Webers on the FWE Climax it must be turning out around 105 bhp in its 900 lb, so the acceleration is quick and feels it as you go up through the close-ratio BMC A-series gearbox; the performance is initially magnified as you sit so close to the road. As a 1962 car, the tyre size options are 4.50 × 15-in or 4.50 × 13-in at front and 5.00 × 15-in or 5.25 × 13-in at the rear; so even on 15-in wheels Lolas score against Listers on a tyre width/weight ratio, although the length of the contact patch is also relevant. Increase tyre sizes within historic racing rules to 5.00L × 13-in front and 6.00L × 13-in rear and there is a lot of rubber on the road for a lightweight car.

Certainly the roadholding was excellent, and the suspension is happy to cope with the extra grip without such undesirable side effects as high roll angles; the car rolls very little. The steering is exceptionally light but not so light as to mask the feel of the understeer under power; lift off and you get a controllable oversteer. The tyres, incidentally, run at 19 psi front and 17 psi rear with an almost 50/50 weight distribution.

The car points well into a corner even if it isn't terribly responsive to wheel movements once in it. Basically, it inspired instant confidence, although the back wheels were inclined to skitter across the track on bumpy Becketts. Ostroumoff used 7500-8000 rpm when racing, but as he was racing again the following day I was a little more cautious. Even limiting myself to 6000 rpm for the first few laps around the Silverstone Club circuit, I was easily down to 1 min 17 sec and another five seconds came off with an extra 1000 rpm. Harder use of the excellent brakes contributed as well, a nice firm pedal encouraging ever later use with an easy heel and toe action on the pedals.

Solidly mounted, the engine was delightful with just about enough torque for a traffic light take off, but beyond 5000 rpm it really flew and smoothly too—you can feel high-frequency vibrations but more as a result of noise than any out-of-balance forces. The FWA/E Climaxes always were lovely little engines and Climax Engine Services obviously know how to keep them that way.

So what had I learnt in answer to the original question—why could Lolas beat Listers? In a period of rapid development, or increasing understanding

Last of the Lola Mk. Is, BR32 (Rupert Glydon) leads BR31 (Mike Ostroumoff) in 1976

of vehicle dynamics, the Lola was almost a generation ahead. The suspension really worked properly, and there was more than enough rubber on the road for the weight to give higher cornering forces and braking, which was effective and consistent with much less heat to dissipate. By its long-distance ability, it also proved that longevity with performance is more likely to be achieved with less weight than more power.

At this point one can't help wondering if the appeal of Le Mans didn't have as stultifying an effect on design during the 1950s as did the TT in the motor-cycle field, but it depends on what the design was for. Jaguar wanted to win Le Mans, Lola didn't.

It has often been argued that Eric Broadley was the founder of the modern Grand Prix rear suspension design with the 1958 Mk. I Lola. Cooper had his transverse leaf and a wishbone, Lotus had the modified Macpherson strut, while the rest had rather heavy de Dion tubes, curiously at a time when racing tyres were much more tolerant of camber angles than they are now.

The difference lay in the radius arm which formed part of a wide-angle wishbone; in fact its transverse link was the fixed length drive shaft with a pair of Hooke-type joints. With that Broadley obviated the problems of spline-lock (which can freeze the suspension until torque is released on the gearchange) and of the sudden tread-wipe on a mid-corner bump (which has the effect of increasing slip angles and reducing grip).

Chapman also used a radius arm plus drive shaft on the Lotus 12, 15 and early 16, but as a lower link with the strut performing the rest of the location. Broadley's lower links, each side of his own upright, were a pair of cross-braced, almost transverse, links to control steering toe movements. Inboard Alfin-type ex-TR drum brakes mean that one trailing arm is adequate, as there is no rotating force on the hub. The modern rear suspension systems use twin trailing arms, usually a single upper link and a pair of lower ones, each joint adjustable where Broadley's were all rubber bushed.

At the front, a Herald-type upright is located on twin wishbones, their apex forward to make the forward links almost transverse while the rear links trail to resist braking torques; brakes are from the Triumph TR2 with Alfin drums. A BMC rack and pinion gives the nice high geared steering and a straight run from wheel to pinion ensures consistent messages.

For the chassis a full width two-tier space frame is well-braced across to give plenty of rigidity for a light weight; the driver is balanced by a fuel tank on the left of the scuttle. In fact no great compromise was required to achieve the equal weight distribution, as the driver's feet are level with the rear of the engine; it is just that the Climax unit is so light — just over 200 lb — while the cast-iron cased A-series gearbox is in the middle and the other mass, the final drive, is carried in a Lola alloy casting.

The neat bodies for the prototype and the 1959 cars were built by Maurice Gomm in aluminium with a fixed scuttle, but the 1960 bodies were in glassfibre from Specialised Mouldings with a one-piece bonnet including the screen, and a one-piece tail, both hinged at their extremities for maximum accessibility.

'The fire pump that wins races' was a descriptive slogan at the time of the birth of the FWA Climax engine. Conceived to a Ministry of Defence requirement during the early days of the Korean war, the 'featherweight' engine started life with 1020 cc developing 36 bhp at 3500 rpm; with aluminium block and head it was very light and efficient, with its overhead camshaft operating inclined in-line valves via bucket tappets — the combustion chamber was a wedge head which gave a good compromise between overall weight and the ultimate efficiency of twin camshafts. This engine ran as early as 1951, but it wasn't until 1954 that it became available as a racing engine, by which time Coventry Climax had already embarked on the still-born FPE V-8 for the 2½-litre Formula 1 as a prestige exercise.

Designers Hassan and Mundy settled for 72·4 × 66·7 mm, 1098 cc dimensions for their little 'four', gave it a steel crankshaft and selected appropriate cam profiles and port design; with an 8·8:1 compression ratio and twin SUs its first output was

The neat and functional cockpit of the Lola, bare of any excess weight

64 bhp at 6000 rpm. By the time Kieft gave it the first public appearance at Le Mans in 1954, they had 72 bhp at 6100 rpm; then the Mk. II the following year was producing 83 bhp at 6800 rpm for a mere £250.

By 1956 with the new F2 in the offing for 1957, Climax introduced a limited run of FWB engines, stretching the engine to its maximum with 76·2 × 80 mm, 1460 cc, but, with the same head and manifolds, peak power was only up to 100 bhp at 6000 rpm, although the torque improvement was noticeable. The 1½-litre FPF twin-cam came in during 1957, but FW production was continued when Chapman wanted a version for the Lotus Elite; 1216 cc came from the FWB bore and the FWA crankshaft to become the FWE developing 72 bhp at 6100 rpm with a single SU on 10:1 compression, or 83 bhp on twin SUs, but racing versions on twin Webers approached 100 bhp at somewhat higher revs. By the time the Elite had finished some 1988 FW engines had been produced including 697 FWA, 35 FWB, and a balance of FWEs (including around 150 for Jack Brabham's Sprite and Herald conversions).

Meanwhile Eric Broadley and his cousin Graham had been competing in 750 Motor Club 1172 events with their cycle-winged special using the old Ford side-valve engine; they won the championship and the Chapman cup in 1957 against such as the Lotus 9s and 11s. With 1100 cc racing going well with more Lotuses, Coopers, Elvas, Tojeiros and the like, Eric Broadley joined the fold with his first car in July 1958, built in a Bromley garage. Unplaced in its maiden outing at Crystal Palace among bigger machinery, the car took second in the 1100 cc race at Snetterton, Eric Broadley at the helm. Brands Hatch in August saw it lap the short circuit in under a minute, an unlimited capacity sports car record; he won his heat but didn't finish in the final. A fastest lap came at Goodwood, although Broadley overturned when contesting the lead. At the TT Broadley/Gammon had to repair a puncture, as they had no spare wheels, but still took the fastest lap in the class although they finished well down the order.

At the end of that year, Eric Broadley gave up his engineering job and formed Lola Cars. Four more cars were built in 1959 at Gomm's Byfleet works, BY1 going to Alan Ross in the USA (with a headfairing), BY2 for Peter Ashdown (works driver), BY3 to Mike Taylor and BY4 to Bernard Cox. The cars soon dominated 1100 cc racing with a 1, 2, 3 at Goodwood and at the Aintree 200, a 1, 2 at the International Trophy and so on. Ashdown and Broadley went to the Nürburgring 1000 Km in June, but unfortunately Broadley was disqualified for receiving outside assistance after a spin, when they were leading the class and well up in the race overall. Ashdown then won at Clermont-Ferrand, beating many larger cars, and won the 1100 class at

Lola Mk. I BR31 is a 1962 car, and thus has 13-inch wheels and disc brakes. The 1220 cc Climax engine produced some 105 bhp

Rouen, running fourth in a 2-litre race. Mike Taylor sold his car to Alan Rees who continued the Lola domination.

Returning to the TT with three cars this time, Ashdown and Alan Ross took sixth overall and the 1100 class, while the three cars took the team prize. It had been a good season, so much so that the works Lola stood alongside the championship winning Aston Martin at the Racing Car Show.

Such were the orders for the new cars that Broadley moved into Rob Rushbrook's Bromley garage and the chassis prefixes changed to BR, running on from the first four; nineteen Bromley cars were produced in 1960, one of them (BR13) for use as a road car for Peter Gourlay with a 1216 cc Elite engine.

Success continued on the home front but the little cars went further overseas this time with an entry at Sebring for Ashdown/Vogele/Rothe using Charles Vogele's red and white car fitted with the tall Appendix C screen; despite losing its bonnet at one stage it still won the 1100 cc class and finished 17th overall. Nürburgring saw it win the 1100 class again from another two Lolas, but Le Mans proved less successful when a piston failed after 17 hours depriving them of the class victory.

Ample confirmation of the Lola's ability came in the British Grand Prix meeting at Silverstone when Ashdown lapped in 1 min 46 sec, all but 100 mph, to finish fourth overall ahead of a number of Listers, and on only 1098 cc. That year, Lolas had a 1, 2 in the BRSCC Sports Car Championship with Ashdown winning from Rees.

For 1961 another batch of cars was built to take the score up to BR29 and Lolas continued their winning ways including a 1, 2, 3, in class at Nürburgring, victory in the Johore Coronation Grand Prix with Chan Lye Choon's 1216 cc BR24, and the Leinster Trophy with Tommy Hayden.

The final season of production saw three more cars, but fitted with disc brakes, while BR30 had a Ford twin-cam unit for Dr Wyllie in America. The *Autosport* Sports Car championship provided a natural playground for the Lolas and they won the 1100 class from 1962-4, very much in the mid-engined period, a remarkable performance over five years of rapid design change.

Eric Broadley's first car marked the end of the front-engined leviathan sports-racing cars, as a triumph of roadholding over brute power; the next generation were to equate the two more effectively with the tyre makers providing the catalyst.

Eric Broadley in the prototype Lola Mk I at the 1958 Goodwood TT, where a puncture delayed the car

AC Cobra

Like most people fond of the ever-faster sports cars of the 1960s, I have a great admiration for the Cobras not only for their good record around the tracks of the world—1965 Manufacturers Sports Car Champions amongst many other victories—but from road driving as well. I remember picking up the *Motor* road test AC 289 from Thames Ditton and immediately driving off for 200 miles to nowhere and back, because it was such a fun car, fast, a little raucous and very controllable. It was my task, too, a little later to pick up John Woolfe's 7-litre and aquaplane home at 50 mph on very fat pock-marked slicks—the only car on which I have run out of fuel twice within 10 miles as I thought I could nurse the car 13 miles on the first gallon can! Perhaps the best Cobra racing memory was seeing Jack Sears taking Jackie Stewart's lightweight E on the outside of Paddock Bend at Brands Hatch after making a controversial black flag stop; Sears was more than a little upset about the stop and subsequently drove in a scarcely controlled cold rage that kept the Willment Cobra on the skittering limit in a masterly display that Jack may never have achieved thereafter in saner moments. He took a new class lap record!

The chance to drive a quick one—the ex-Chequered Flag one at that—at Goodwood was not to be missed. Actually, it nearly was missed as the car was a little late turning up, because the mechanic couldn't get the rev counter to work, and I nearly had to make do with the 1966 lightweight Ferrari GTB in which the owner, Martin Hilton, had driven up!

They never did get the rev counter to work and, since the speedometer was disconnected, it was a case of blind flying on a circuit I didn't know that well. The last time I had driven there had been in a Lotus 15, which was so low that I never really got the hang of what went on over the brows that you don't notice in something as relatively high as a Cobra. I took my road car round for a few laps first to give me a better idea of lines and braking points, but since I never knew how fast I was going in the Cobra it wasn't that relevant, although better brakes and roadholding meant that braking points were surprisingly similar.

It's a brutal looking beast, dark blue with widely flared wings, aggressive jutting grille-less intake with the square oil cooler intake below, flanked by big holes to feed air to massive discs, side exhausts, roll-over bar—squat and purposeful. This was a leaf-sprung car developed from the old AC with a stronger chassis; that means transverse leaf and wishbones all round.

The driving position is fairly cramped even for my average frame and I found heel and toe operation very awkward with the existing pedal spacing and long throttle travel. It's an easy starter and a noisy runner but tractable enough pottering across the paddock; the engine is a 5-litre Gurney-Weslake headed Ford which has plenty of power all the way up, so the loss of a few hundred revs for

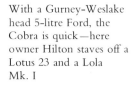

With a Gurney-Weslake head 5-litre Ford, the Cobra is quick—here owner Hilton staves off a Lotus 23 and a Lola Mk. I

The thoroughly mas-
culine controls and cock-
pit of a racing Cobra

caution's sake didn't really affect one's impressions. Inevitably, with no rev counter, early laps were gentle but, knowing that the gearing allowed full throttle all the way down the Lavant straight, I tried to use the ultimate noise level attained there as a suitable aural rev limit elsewhere—it's still together so I can't have been too far out. The noise is impressive, a sort of deep thunderous crashing sound as a mixture of engine thrash, intake roar and exhaust bellow made more so with the full width screen in use.

Everything about the car is heavy; the big close ratio box with its lever offset to the left (an American box) requires very firm and deliberate movements, the clutch needs a solid prod and the brakes like a lot of weight, while the steering with 5.50M × 15-in tyres on the directional end requires and develops a powerful pair of forearms. But it is sensitive and you can really feel what the front end is doing as it begins to wash out on the exit from the fast Fordwater, the only place you can come out of the corner without sufficient power surplus to bring in the oversteer and where there isn't another corner immediately afterwards to require forward planning. On the straights, it walks about a bit as the big tyres nibble at the surface variations, but you soon forget that.

Power surplus is what the Cobra is all about—it's there in abundance—but the chassis seems well up to it. Establish a constant speed limit for a corner, then nudge the throttle for the required degree of directional change for the correct exit line, without applying speed scrubbing lock. The tail moves out surprisingly gently and you can apply full throttle the moment that the front wheels are straight; it was useful to do this in the St Mary's left hander dip where the adverse camber encourages the nose to run wide and it was fun, if less useful out of Woodcote, where a quick burst of throttle is followed by a lunge on the brakes for the chicane.

On most of the circuit the suspension worked well with the feel of a giant go-kart on an almost billiard-table surface—firm but no bounce—but I noticed some front-end lurch in the earlier part of Woodcote, where you have just come off the brakes and are gradually putting the power in for the second half of the apex. Not enough to upset the line but there all the same to show that the suspension wasn't perfect.

In its racing heyday a Goodwood time was around 1 min 27 sec; in recent sprints on a deteriorating surface with fewer marker boards, Martin Hilton reckons on 1 min 34 sec; blind flying I was happy with 1 min 37 sec which could have been faster or slower with a rev counter and, perhaps, better with a more reliable heel and toe.

This particular Cobra was built for C. T. 'Tommy' Atkins and had its first race at that 1964 British GP meeting where Jack Sears did his balancing act; in fact, Salvadori was on pole in the Atkins car, still unpainted, and he finished third. Chris Amon was next one out in the car at the August Bank Holiday meeting and just lost to Sears. At the Goodwood TT Salvadori was out again and had a late modification made to the front end to cure high speed lift; he was leading the GT category for the first 50 laps ahead of the Shelby-entered coupes but dropped out; it was Dan Gurney who achieved fastest lap in the coupe at 1 min 27·8 sec.

At the end of the 1964 season the car was sold to Graham Warner's Chequered Flag at which point it was registered for the first time as GPG 4C which is why a 1964 car carries a 1965 number.

It was sorted to its maximum extent at Chequered Flag with a Holman and Moody engine. At that time Graham Warner was entering quite a few youngish drivers like Roy Pike, Roger Mac, Bob Bondurant, Chris Irwin and they all had their hands on this wheel; the 1965 Guards Trophy meeting saw Bondurant give it a third, after leading

Following pages: Hilton's Cobra contrasts with a 1966 lightweight Ferrari 275GTB

Jack Sears won the GT race at the 1964 British GP meeting, despite a brief pit stop in response to the black flag. This was a Willment Cobra

most of the GT race, letting Sears past when the engine lost song. Roger Mac had been driving it at Goodwood and took the Goodwood Trophy the year after he had won the premier Grovewood award. It was sad that at the end of that year Tommy Atkins died.

Come 1966 and Ford GT40s were everywhere, Graham Warner had a 7-litre Cobra as well as the 4·7-litre so this one wasn't used that much. It nearly achieved a second in the very wet Ilford Films 500-mile race in the hands of Pike/Irwin behind the winning Piper/Bondurant 7-litre, but dropped a rod before the end.

The car then passed to Shaun Jackson who had several successful club seasons with it before selling it to Wendy Hamblin. Martin Hilton bought it from Brian Classic; Mathwall Engineering rebuilt the engine to the Gurney–Weslake specification, although the Hiltons have subsequently rebuilt it and it certainly goes extremely well now, an excellent example of a great car.

Chronologically the AC story has to start in 1900 but suffice to say that by 1950, the Thames Ditton firm had a long history behind them, producing some stylish saloons and tourers as well as some interesting sprint and record cars. And in 1919 one of the original partners, John Weller, designed a single overhead camshaft six-cylinder 2-litre which was to last through to 1954, a life-span which Jaguar have yet to surpass.

The year 1950 saw John Tojeiro build the first of a number of specials which were to use MG TC, Lea-Francis and JAP engines. Then for 1952 he built the Tojeiro-Bristol which was to form the basis of the new AC Ace; clothing it in a body resembling the Ferrari 166MM Barchetta, he produced a car that was very successful on the tracks in the hands of Cliff Davis and deserved to be marketed. Thus the

1953 Motor Show saw the prototype AC on display, the Tojeiro reproduced, now trimmed, and powered by the AC 2-litre engine.

Tojeiro had obviously studied form and chosen the best of all thoughts, a stiff ladder-type tubular frame with all-round independent suspension with an attractive lightweight aluminium body. The transverse upper leaf spring with a wishbone below had been used on pre-war cars (BMW, DKW, Fiat) for the front end—and after the war by Cooper at both ends; this was what Tojeiro adopted, adding Alfin-style drum brakes, an ENV final drive with AC engine and gearbox.

The new Ace was in production for 1954 and proved an immediate success on road and track where Ken Rudd was particularly impressive.

It was Ken Rudd who persuaded the Hurlocks, who had owned AC since 1930, to offer the Bristol engine with its 140 bhp potential as an option alongside the 85 bhp Ace; this was taken up in 1956, and Rudd and others continued their success, which was being repeated on the American side of the Atlantic. Disc brakes were added to the specification in 1957.

Production of the Bristol engine ceased in 1960 and it was Ken Rudd who assisted the choice of the 2·6-litre Ford Zephyr engine as its replacement, mated to a Moss-type gearbox with overdrive; this could produce up to 170 bhp with an alloy head and triple Webers, and the car was still quite happy to take the extra weight and power in substantially the original form.

Meanwhile Carroll Shelby, having made his racing name in Europe with Aston Martin, wanted to create his own road and track sports car with real performance. Hearing that the Bristol engine was no longer being produced, and that the Ford 2·6-litre hadn't really succeeded as the replacement, he decided that the Ace body/chassis was ideal to take an American V-8. The Hurlocks agreed and Shelby talked Ford into producing a thin-wall cast-iron V–8 221 cu in engine; by the time this became available it was a 260 cu in (4·2-litre) unit that was to go into the first Cobras, the name that Shelby had, literally, dreamt up. The first chassis went out to Shelby in California in 1962 where they were fitted with the 4·2-litre engine and gearbox.

The first 75 AC Cobras had the small engine and used worm and sector steering; with the Mk. II came the 4·7-litre engine and a larger radiator while 50 cars later came rack and pinion steering—altogether 650 Mk. IIs were built with the last one delivered in December 1966, although the Americans had stopped receiving them in September 1964.

The reason for this was the birth of the 7-litre Mk. III for which the chassis understandably required a complete revamp; this was provided by the Ford computer, which uprated the main tube section from 3 to 4 in and designed full wishbone/coil spring suspension all-round. It was shatteringly quick with some 425 bhp in standard form or over 500 bhp in Holman and Moody racing trim—some 320 7-litre Mk. IIIs were sold in America, but when that came to an end in the face of USA legislation, AC continued to sell the Mk. III in England and Europe, with the 4·7-litre from 1966-69 (this accounted for another 30 cars).

In racing terms the Shelby AC Cobras did well in America from the moment they arrived, but with the introduction of the 4·7-litre the output was beginning to make them potential Ferrari challengers. However the bluff front and open screen of the standard cars was hardly the most streamlined vehicle in which to go serious racing against the might of Maranello, who were still using the GTO, having failed to get the 250LM homologated. So Pete Brock was commissioned to style a fixed head coupe version in late 1963; this was completed in early 1964, adding an extra 15 mph in top speed. It was vindicated at Daytona where the car led for seven hours against the Ferraris before retiring, and the new style was immediately christened the Daytona Coupe. Mounting for the body was around a tubular frame-work which also served to stiffen the Mk. II chassis, still on transverse leaf springs.

Although the Cobras did well in 1964, finishing with the first three GT places in the TT, they were still pipped by Ferrari for the GT Manufacturers championship. In 1965, Ford set out for the prototype championship with the GT40s, but they also wanted to win the GT races, so Alan Mann was asked to run the team. This time the FIA wouldn't homologate Ferrari's latest production car, the 275GTB until Le Mans as they couldn't agree a weight, so the Cobras were still fighting against private GTOs, but this time they won; Detroit iron had finally beaten Maranello refinement.

By 1966 Ford had homologated the GT40, so the 7-litre Cobra wasn't needed on the International race tracks and that was that; Shelby had gone on to look after the GT40s and Cobra production for America ceased that year. Arguably it was the last real GT car that was close to anything that could be used on the road by anyone, and it was certainly the last time that a small company like AC would win a major championship for anything but outright track cars.

Le Mans in 1964 saw the Daytona Cobra of Gurney and Bondurant finish fourth, and beat the Ferrari 250GTOs. But they had to wait a year to take the championship

Aston Martin Project 212

Always known as Project 212, Aston Martin's 1962 official title was DP (Design project) 212. As such it was a sort of test-bed for the DB5 and was very much what the Le Mans organisers had in mind when they added a category for genuine prototypes of up to 4 litres, to race alongside the official FIA World Championship of Makes for GT cars. Success in the long-distance classic would be a good launching pad for Aston technology, relating to both the DB5 and the Lagonda Rapide.

There's something about an old Le Mans racer; it has all sorts of little appendages peculiar to that great long-distance classic. Lights over the number circles, tags for sealing filler caps, provision for fresh air for the driver, extra light switches, massive fuel tanks and readily accessible fuse boxes are items you get in a Le Mans racer which you don't get in the usual short-distance GT car. Project 212 was typical with a battery of switches and dials to daunt the unfamiliar driver. Since it had been tailored to Mike Salmon, who has driven it most over the years, the seat was fixed for rather over 6 ft of driver, which meant I had to make use of a multi-folded blanket both underneath and behind me to let me see out and reach the pedals; the four-strap harness clamped me adequately to maintain control.

To manage a track test of the 1974 Classic Car Championship winner I had to take part in the official practice for one of the 'other' races at Aintree which was just before Salmon took part in the final race of the series, so I wasn't about to set any great pace.

Project 212 starts easily as long as you get the engine turning over before flicking on the ignition switch. Once fired up it can tick over quite happily without oiling up, but blipping the throttle produces that superb Aston baying blast of sound; once out on the circuit, with crash helmet on, you don't really notice the sounds, particularly at Aintree's Club Circuit where corners come up with a rapidity that is totally mind-consuming for the uninitiated. I hadn't been there before, so concentrated particularly hard to ensure the continued existence of this famous car. I also kept to 5500 rpm instead of 6000 rpm just in case the gear lever should prove reluctant to accept the right slot at the right time; it didn't and snicked around its five-speed gate (fifth on its own) with a precision that belied its racing miles.

Despite a bulky appearance 212 weighs around a ton and with 350 bhp/ton it accelerates accordingly; it is fast and feels it. Although it is tractable enough at intermediate revs it begins to get on song beyond 4000 rpm and really pulls away from 5000 rpm.

The pedals sprout from the floor in classic Aston fashion and all three require firm pressure, but since it is very much a he-man sort of car, such movement never unbalances you. The steering is heavy too; it is responsive and you can feel the front end picking up the surface variations as you brake, but once the power is on, any initial understeer disappears and the throttle eases the steering effort; on tighter corners the attitude is very much a function of throttle which even I could usefully use when lining up for the 60 degree Village right-hander after the 90 degree left of Country — badly cambered too the first one, while Village has some banking to help. Mike Salmon uses the right-footed attitude control rather more reasily, and was coming through the long 180 degree Club in a manner more reminiscent

Aston Martin Project DP212 at speed in 1974, with Mike Salmon driving for Lord Downe. This was a genuine prototype for a road-going car, and not a Le Mans special

of John Rhodes in a Mini than one appropriate to a Grand Tourer—the tail would start to come round half way through the corner and the car would be pointing the way required for the next straight some time before it got there, with the opposite lock being killed the moment the straight was ahead. It is remarkable to see such a large car displaying such agility. In fact Salmon, who did a lot of Aston development testing, reckons that 214 has better front end grip and will get through such a corner faster as it can take more power for a given attitude. It felt fast enough for me in a neutral condition.

If I had known the circuit beforehand, I might have enjoyed it even more but a new car on a new circuit, with Mike Salmon peering over your shoulder waiting to drive afterwards, is fairly daunting, but it was a great experience to drive such a car, not least because it is still very much in its Le Mans trim and owner Lord Downe has deliberately kept it that way without falling prey to the temptations of adding modernity in the shape of even wider wheels and appropriate wheel arch flares. Richard Williams now maintains it and it goes as well as ever but more reliably—the racing miles of 1974 alone would have taken it further through Le Mans than it managed in 1962!

Aston Martin had pulled out of racing at the end of the DBR1/2/3 and single-seater DBR4 season of 1959, but continued to supply customers with the DB4GT in British and Zagato forms for privateer racing and even to prepare the cars for them.

Project 212 was announced just before Le Mans

1962 for drivers Graham Hill and Ritchie Ginther. It was announced with the subsequently familiar dimensions of 96 × 92 mm, 3996 cc; Aston Martin were 'not out to compete against other prototypes just to extend the normal testing of experimental cars' according to *Autocar*. So 212 was a large car capable of carrying back seat passengers had it ever reached production; the wheelbase was just an inch longer than the DB4GT at 7 ft 10 in while the overall length at 14 ft 6 in was 6 in up on the Zagato-like with a slightly upswept underside to the Zagato's. In its 1962 form 212's tail was very Zagato-like with a slightly unswept underside which was to prove unstable at Mulsanne speeds.

With a quoted dry weight of 2150 lb it was some 400 lb lighter than a Zagato which was basically a DB4GT production car with an Italian outer skin. The reduction was achieved by using a normal-looking but drilled rectangular box section chassis with aluminium floor panels, while the body was carefully beaten in 20 swg magnesium/aluminium alloy panels at the Tickford factory at Newport Pagnell where Aston Martin had yet to move.

While the standard seven-bearing 'six' had 92 × 92 mm dimensions for 3670 cc and the factory had prepared engines with 93 mm for 3750 cc, 212 had a 4 mm overbore to take it out to nearly 4 litres, although the Le Mans programme had it down as 3749 cc! Somehow Aston Martin always caught themselves out on their power figures and the quoted 345 bhp at 6000 rpm was optimistic—it was actually 330 bhp: however 212 featured 50DCO Webers and the twin-plug head developed for the

Le Mans cars always have more equipment than others—Project 214's cockpit has a range of switchgear and a large fresh air 'eyeball'

GTs with an 80 degree valve angle modified for the bigger bore with a 9·6:1 compression. The original output for a normal DB4 on twin SUs was 240 bhp at 5500 rpm.

It was run with a David Brown five-speed gearbox in a magnesium alloy casing with a 3·27 final drive (2·91 fifth). Front suspension used double wishbones and coil springs, but a de Dion system was used at the rear with torsion bar springing, using trailing arms and a Watt linkage.

Come the race and the car went well in practice and at the start was almost first away, overtaking a Corvette before the Dunlop bridge and leading the race for a lap; at the end of the first hour it was second but a change of dynamo armature delayed it before an oil pump supply pipe fractured and that was that after five hours. In fact it was reassembled in time for Monday morning demonstrations to the press who were suitably impressed.

After this 212 returned to Feltham and didn't even turn out for the TT to accompany the two Ogier Zagatos and Salmon's Zagato. Not much of a post-mortem was needed—high speed stability and an avoidance of oil pipe fractures. Spoilers and Kamm tails had become fashionable and proven effective, so when 1963 Le Mans practice week-end came round 212 had grown a flat-back and spoiler.

In addition a pair of DB4GTs had been built up with lighter versions of the standard chassis—well drilled box section frame with aluminium flooring and a standard suspension layout, albeit with more adjustability. These were DP214 cars—0194 and 0195. Both were fitted with the 1 mm overbore capacity of 3750 cc but differed in the heads with 0194 having straight ports, 50DCO carburettors with 9·15 compression ratio while 0195 had a standard GT head with 9·3 compression ratio and 45DCOE Webers. Outputs were 310 bhp at 6000 rpm and 300 bhp at 5800 rpm respectively. With oil and water the 214s weighed 2121 lb and 212 heavier at 2280 lb. The 214 bodies featured the same tail arrangement as 212 but had a longer nose and a smaller air intake.

Some trouble was experienced with the 214s which suffered from oil surge under braking and they were later fitted with hinged-baffle sumps. The 7HA axles were running up to 130°C and were changed later for the older 4HA axle. Ex-DBR1 combined oil/water radiators were not effective enough on the 214s but the E-type radiator worked well on 212. Excessive understeer on all cars was countered with a small front anti-roll bar for the 214s while 212 had its rear roll centre lowered from an inch above hub height to an inch below for the same effect—this contradicts accepted theory but apparently worked. All the cars were running on 6L/6½L × 16-in front/rear wheels experimenting with R5 and R6 Dunlops up to 7.00 × 16 R5s on the rear. Ginther had a run in 212 and confirmed that the car was better than in the previous year, with improved stability but not a lot faster in maximum speed; the 214s with less power were as fast and some 11 mph faster than the Zagatos of 1962.

Meanwhile work had already started on DP215; this used a new chassis of similar concept but with greater rigidity provided by a central cruciform. The front suspension followed the previous double wishbone design, but the rear was completely new with again a double wishbone set-up coupled with a rear-mounted DBR-type five-speed transaxle. This gave a hub height roll centre but was only adjustable for camber and toe-in. The engine was similar to that of 212 with the 3996 capacity but used a dry sump lubrication system; after the test week-end all three engines used small throat GT heads and 50DCO Webers with 0·51/0·45-in lift of inlet and exhaust cams. This gave 215 more mid-range torque than 212 had had, with two 290 lb/ft humps at 4600 and 5500 rpm where 212 had a peak of 287 lb/ft at 5300 rpm; its output was slightly down at 326 bhp at 5800 rpm; the two 214s now produced 314 and 310 bhp for 0194 and 0195.

Drivers were Phil Hill/Lucien Bianchi in 215 with McLaren/Ireland in 0194 and Kimberley/Schlesser in 0195; during practice the 214 cars behaved well and 215 was gradually sorted with toe-in and camber changes at the rear, finally getting down to 3 min 52·0 sec against the fastest by Rodriguez' Ferrari. The 214s had got down to 3 min 58·7 sec in April and had recorded a best of 4 min 00 sec in official practice; both Ireland and 215 had recorded 300 kph on the Mulsanne straight. The race plan was for 215 to lap at 4 min 5 sec and the 214s at 4 min 15 sec.

In the race Hill led away in 215 but dropped back to a comfortable fifth after 4 laps; a Rene-Bonnet crashed just over the Dunlop bridge hill on Hill's sixth lap and he ran over some of the debris stopping to check for chassis damage. He was back up to ninth place by the refuelling stop at 26 laps but when Bianchi took over the transmission failed as the teeth on the input bevel gear had failed. Since this had never happened on the DBR cars it assumed that the extra torque of the 4-litre had contributed.

Meanwhile the 214s were running to plan and at 28 laps McLaren stopped for fuel when leading the GT class and 10th overall. Ireland took it up to sixth overall in his stint but a piston failed after 60 laps when McLaren was speeding down the Mulsanne straight; the resultant oil caused considerable confusion, one of the spinners being the Kerguen/Franc Zagato which was later to retire with a seized axle. Having stopped after three laps to unblock a main jet, the other 214 had more luck and worked up to fifth overall after 110 laps—nearly eight hours. By 10 hours it was lying third and leading the GT class but that car too suffered a piston failure, so that was that for Aston Martin's final Le Mans. It was decided that the piston failure was due to inadequate strength around the underside of the gudgeon-pin boss.

Jo Schlesser drove 215 at Rheims in the 25-lap GT race accompanying the French GP. He had had considerable difficulty with gear changing on the five-speed box and frequently missed gears; valves were hit beyond 6800 rpm, although the bottom end proved itself capable of withstanding at least 7200 rpm. In the race Schlesser managed to lead on the first lap but having missed three gears in four laps retired with bent valves.

Classic twin-cam 'six' in
the Aston Martin Project
212, which is stretched to
4·2 litres in its present
form; note the twin-plug
head

Although 215's handling at Le Mans was satisfactory, at Rheims Schlesser was finding the front end too light on the fast right hander after the pits, which led to the conclusion that the weight distribution was wrong. DP212 had its engine in more or less Zagato position with 1309 lb on the front for a 51·9/48·1 weight distribution. The 214s had the engines back some 8½ in for 1218 lb on the front but a similar distribution (51·4/48·6) — de Dion tubes are heavy. However with 215 the engine was a further 1½ in back which gave 1176 lb on the front for 47·5/52·5 distribution.

DP215 was to have been driven at Brands Hatch in the Guards trophy, but McLaren had been injured in the German GP and Kimberley just demonstrated the car. However Kimberley did finish sixth in 0194 but Ireland retired in 0195. After this 215 had an accident on the M1 and stayed at Aston Martin as a kit of parts for some time; Colin Crabbe had the engine and transmission when he owned 0194, and the engine went with that car to its present owner.

However, as GTs the two 214s continued and took part in the Goodwood Tourist Trophy with Ireland in 0194 and McLaren in 0195. The cars had now been developed to run on their 6½/6-in rims, but Aston Martin had only homologated the 6-in ones so the cars were rejected until the old rims were

At Le Mans in 1964 Mike Salmon rounds Mulsanne in the DB4GT-based DP214 Aston. It was disqualified for taking on oil too soon

replaced; this is said to have accounted for Ireland's spins! He started dicing with Hill's Maranello GTO for the lead but they touched and spun, which sent Ireland back to the pits for unflatted tyres; a subsequent touch and spin with Parkes' Ferrari dropped him further down the field to finish seventh. McLaren's car was consuming too much oil with tappet troubles and leaky sump gasket and was retired.

The two 214s made their final works sortie with a visit to Monza for the GT race accompanying the Italian GP, and to Montlhéry on the return journey. At Monza, Salvadori drove 0194 to victory ahead of Parkes' Ferrari while Bianchi was third in 0195 ahead of David Piper's Ferrari. Both cars were using 310 bhp units.

At Montlhéry the Coupe de Paris was open to GT cars and 2-litre sports prototypes; after Dauwe's Lotus had lost its transmission the two 214s gained a 1, 2 with Claude Le Guezec finishing five seconds ahead of Dewez. In the coupe de Salon Schlesser won in 0195 with Le Guezec fifth.

That was the swansong of Aston's works involvement and at the end of the year the two 214s and 212 were up for sale. Mike Salmon and Brian Hetreed had created Atherstone Engineering and acquired the 214s. The Hon John Dawnay—now Viscount Downe—joined in to enter the cars under a Dawnay Racing banner and bought 212 with a view to turning it into a road car. It was registered AYN 212B and supplied by the factory with a 4164 cc engine, 98 mm bore, giving 349 bhp at 6000 rpm.

The conversion of 212 to road use didn't get very far although it was certainly used as such, as well as having outings in 1964 at Wiscombe Hill Climb, Silverstone and Brighton Speed Trials where Salmon recorded 24·45 sec. Salmon also drove it in the *Autosport* three-hour race at Snetterton but the final drive failed. The two 214s were to be

campaigned in International GT events with Salmon in 0194 and Hetreed in 0195.

Both went to the Daytona 2000 km with Salmon partnered by Salvadori and Hetreed with Kerrison; both had been in fifth place during the race but 0194 retired with valve failure and 0195 slipped back to 17th when the gearbox started to seize. At the International Trophy Silverstone GT race Salmon broke the GT record in practice at 1 min 41·0 sec but spun in the wet on the first lap and then worked back through the field to take second behind Hill's Maranello 1964 GTO. Spa for the 500 km saw both cars in engine trouble with no results. Both went to the Nürburgring 1000 km but Brian Hetreed was killed in a practice accident and 0195 was written off, its engine being transferred later to a Zagato.

The team had taken 212 out while 0194 was being prepared for Le Mans but understandably they went home without racing and the next outing was at Le Mans where Salmon was partnered by Sutcliffe, but they were disqualified after 17¾ hours for taking on oil at the wrong time when lying 11th. The closing events of the season saw Salmon fifth in the Silverstone Martini meeting, and first GT with a fastest lap in 1 min 42·8 sec, and fourth in class in the Guards Trophy despite a spin at Clearways.

After an expensive attempt to keep the Aston name still going in International competition, Dawnay Racing sold 0194 but kept 212 in retirement. It was given occasional airings mostly at Aston Martin events and parades but it wasn't until the advent of the post-Historic series which became the Classic Car Championship that the car was brought back to its former glory.

The sole remaining 214 went to Tom Rose, thence to Colin Crabbe, Nick Cussons and Mike Otway. And 215 is being rebuilt around what remained after the accident. So Aston's final racing fling is still well represented with 212 the car that never stopped racing.

Cooper Monaco

Just to sit in a Cooper Monaco after driving one of the front-engined brigade is enough to convince you that it is half-way into another era. It isn't just the short bonnet and the knowledge that your feet are where the engine might be—everything feels lighter; you can move the steering wheel quite easily when at rest, and the gear lever on your right lacks the heavy precision of one in top of a box. Forward, you notice the wheel arches but they are a little below the natural sight-line, which is over rather than through the screen; the mirror on John Harper's red car is set high, so you can see rearwards over a tail which is the same height as the screen top. Pedals are quite nicely spaced and the lack of transmission hump gives you space to put a clutch foot on its own rest—so many cars force you to keep your foot suspended or slid under the pedal.

Starting the $2\frac{1}{2}$-litre Climax FPF was easy enough, but it felt as if all the bearings had gone, so harsh was the vibration—the penalty of a big 'four' with no flywheel. Keeping it blipping didn't seem to ease the problem, but it is remarkable how quickly the sensation disappears once you are moving and the engine is on drive or overrun. And on drive it is certainly an impressive performer, pulling strongly from around 3000 rpm towards 6500 rpm in a steady surge which can leave nominally more powerful cars gasping in the wake of superior torque/weight figures, which are enhanced by the smaller frontal area at the top end.

Steering is light and sensitive and the car seemed to point in well on the overrun with little understeer; as power is fed in the back adjusts its slip angles without feeling as though it is moving across the track; feed in more power though, and it will oversteer, but gradually, to the point that it can be held on almost opposite lock with the power still on—or so Harper tells me, as I didn't reach that point of delicate balance. It never felt as if the tail was permanently poised to take over in one great swing.

Knowing the gearbox was fragile I treated it with suitable deference; there is a fair amount of movement at the lever even when the gear is engaged, but you always find the right cog and it doesn't feel as frail from the cockpit as it is in the casing.

In exploratory lappery the brakes felt quite nice, not too heavy but with a firm pedal and firm response; but as you go faster, to the point where the brakes are still just on as you turn the wheel, the tail suddenly becomes very light—heavy braking in a straight line confirmed that there was just too much braking on the rear wheels; with equal braking front and rear—same calipers, same master cylinders—the forward weight transfer is still enough to overcome the rearward static weight distribution, even with the pedal pivot wound right over to a front bias. So at present it brakes much like a Lister—keep it straight.

I didn't get the chance to drive it on a circuit for which I have Lister times, but it was enough to show that it is right that history should repeat itself; the mid-engined breed is easier to drive and with

Following pages: John Harper in the Cooper Monaco

A standard early Cooper Monaco with transverse leaf spring rear suspension and dumpy bodywork

more potential than the front-engined cars that were struggling to keep up from the 1950s into the early 1960s. Development and reliability kept the front-engined cars to the fore in long-distance races, but the Cooper Monaco and then the Lotus Monte Carlo demonstrated that longevity spells weight and a loss of agility. Successful though the $1\frac{1}{2}$-litre Porsche RS series were, it was the Cooper with its $2\frac{1}{2}$-litre Climax power that really made the point.

Although the mid-engined sports-racing Cooper Monaco wasn't totally pre-eminent in its field, it did, like other Coopers before it, start a trend on which others were to capitalise. It was the transition car, the one that proved that small efficient sports cars could be just as effective against relative leviathans, provided that the engine was at the other end, as were the single-seaters.

The cars of Charles and John Cooper need little introduction. Early on the scene to join the Bristol-based band who founded cheap $\frac{1}{2}$-litre racing, the Coopers were soon in production with the cars that were to become part of the International Formula Three from 1948 to 1958. By that time we had seen front-engined sports cars—Cooper-MG, Cooper-Bristol (better known in single-seater form) and Cooper-Jaguar—and mid-engined Formula 2 single-seaters as well as variants of the original 500s, with 1000 cc twins running in F2 events and in hill-climbs and sprints. And in 1954 we had seen the first mid-engined sports Cooper, the 1100/1500.

Throughout this variety there was a common line, the tubular chassis with independent suspension at both ends by transverse leaf springs and lower wishbones; it came from the Fiat Topolino initially, with two front half-chassis welded together, a solution that occurred to John Cooper after he had already decided to use the Fiat front as a Cooper front.

Although the components were increased in size as time went on the principle remained the same, whether the engine was at the front or behind the driver. That manx-tailed Cooper of 1954 was the first to pose a gearbox problem for Cooper, as all previous models used proprietary units whether from motor cycles or the cars that provided the engines; it was also the start of a long association with Coventry Climax that was to lead to the two World Championships in 1959 and 1960.

The Climax engine had first been raced in a Kieft for the 1954 Le Mans, an 1100 cc FWA with a single overhead camshaft. The thought of installing this 'featherweight' engine in the back of one of the Cooper 500s appealed. With 84 bhp from a longer engine to cope with, a variant of chain drive was obviously impossible so a gearbox had to be found; it came via John Heath, a Citroen dealer as well as HWM manufacturer.

The Citroen Light Fifteen used a three-speed gearbox in front of its engine; a new bellhousing and an inverted crownwheel would adapt it for the Climax but three speeds weren't enough. Jack Knight converted the first gearbox to four speeds with dog-clutch engagement, and subsequent production was in the hands of the Parisian firm of

Ersa who specialised in bolt-on goodies for Citroen.

Rules of the day allowed a central driving position with outrigged passenger seat, so the new car was relatively simple to arrange on 500 cc experience, and its neat Kamm-tailed shape was born from Hawker aircraft knowledge. It had its fair share of success, although Colin Chapman was as ingenious in his use of proprietary components and the Climax engine in an equally slippery body. Soon the FWA grew bigger and up to 1500 cc. By 1956, with regulations requiring two equal seats, a proper two-seater body arrived.

That year too saw the announcement of a new $1\frac{1}{2}$-litre F2 car; the sports 1100 was slimmed down again and ran with the single-cam engine as a prelude to the official F2 restarting in 1957, by which time the Climax FPF was available.

Stretching the FPF to join the Formula One scene saw the gearbox begin to suffer and 1958 saw Ersa produce a stronger casing to take the Cooper internals. The chassis too was beginning to show its weaknesses and at the front wishbones and coil springs replaced the old transverse leaf to cope with disc brakes.

That season saw Cooper take the European F2 championship and finish third in the Constructors' F1 championship to Vanwall and Ferrari; it also saw an extension to the Surbiton works which allowed a return to sports-car thinking. Given that the uprated F2 car could win GPs, John Cooper obviously wanted a sporting equivalent, which the earlier sports car was no longer able to provide with drum brakes—discs optional—and a 1500 Climax FWB. The Cooper Monaco was the result—presumably as a result of Cooper's 1958 GP victory there, although Argentine was really their first win.

Once again the continuous thread of development was evident as the Monaco used engine, transmission and suspension from the 1958 GP cars. Its chassis used four basic longitudinal tubes curving outwards around the two seats; these were of $1\frac{1}{2}$-in diameter. Cross bracing was provided at toe level, scuttle and at the rear bulkhead, extending upwards to provide a roll-hoop and body attachment, although there were separate outrigged body mounting tubes of smaller section at scuttle and rear bulkhead; a further crossmember passed under the bellhousing and another linked the rear of the lower longerons onto which the upper ones curved down. Triangulation was provided to support front and rear suspension upper mounts. It was a neat extension of the single-seater design but probably lacked torsional stiffness with the frame tubes twice as far apart across the cockpit.

For the suspension, the front used upper and lower wishbones with adjustable spherical joints outboard at the top and metal bushes at the bottom; an anti-roll bar ran through the upper front frame tube. The upright was Herald-type with outboard $10\frac{1}{4}$-in diameter Girling discs and Armstrong adjustable coil/damper units were used.

At the rear the lower wishbone was bushed at both ends and fastened to a magnesium-alloy Cooper hub carrier; upper springing and location was through the transverse leaf spring bolted at its centre, but with outboard rollers to provide a nominal rising roll-rate and an effective wishbone length. At the time it is said that there was provision for an upper wishbone and the use of the leaf spring solely as a spring. Wheels were Cooper's well-known cast-spoke alloy variety 4.50 × 15/5.50 or 6.00 × 15 Dunlops at front/rear. Rear discs were outboard and dampers were again Armstrong adjustables.

The FPF engines were four-point mounted on rubber and canted at 18 degrees to the left, giving an awkward run for the two twin-choke SUs that were original equipment. The uprated Ersa box by now featured an interlock which held the selector rod plungers positively in their notches to prevent the dogs being thrown apart due to wear; as this was coupled to the clutch operation, engagement was positive and light as strong plunger springs were no longer needed. The GP cars also had increased oil capacity of the box with a replenishment tank atop the box, driver operated.

Major weights were disposed around the chassis to finish with a driver plus half-tank distribution of 44/56; a combined radiator and oil cooler was mounted at the front with the dry sump oil tank just behind, a fuel tank balanced the driver on the opposite side and the raditor header tank sat on top of the engine. Radiator air found its way out of the front wheel arches.

The whole was enclosed in a glassfibre body, Dzus fastened to the chassis, with tail and bonnet panels hinged at their extremities to the chassis. The tail panel was depressed in the centre to assist rearward vision and scoops each side fed air into the engine compartment.

With 176 bhp available from the 2-litre FPF in a claimed weight (dry) of 1120 lb, even the small engine could produce a power/weight ratio comparable to that of a 280 bhp 1900 lb Lister. Coopers weren't going to run works cars and initially quoted dollar prices of 7700 for the 1½-litre and 8260 for the 2-litre.

Early customers in the 1959 season were the Chequered Flag, whose driver Percy Crabb wrote the car off in its first outing on a wet Snetterton, and Jim Russell, who retired at that meeting complaining of poor wet road handling. John Coombs had another and installed a 2½-litre Maserati 'four'. With Roy Salvadori driving, this was the combination to beat. Meanwhile Lotus had introduced the 15 as the sports version of their GP/F2 car with the engine at the front and were almost as fast. Jack Brabham effectively ran the works Cooper while another went to Chris Bristow.

However the wet British Empire Trophy meeting at Oulton saw Jim Russell win from Salvadori, Hill's 2-litre Lotus, Bueb's Lister and Brabham's Cooper. Came a dry race the following week-end at the Aintree 200 and Salvadori won from Hill with Gregory's Ecosse Lister-Jaguar third.

A fortnight later Graham Hill had a 2½-litre FPF in the Lotus and led the Silverstone International Trophy sports-car race until he retired leaving victory to Salvadori from Moss (Aston DBR1), Bueb's 3-litre Lister-Jaguar and Flockhart's Tojeiro-Jaguar; Brabham was sixth in the 2-litre

Sid Hoole's Cooper Monaco has the 1960 Grand Prix car rear suspension and gearbox which is stronger than in earlier cars

The Zerex Special was the forerunner of the McLaren CanAm cars, based on a single-seater Cooper rather than a Monaco. Here Bruce McLaren leads Jim Clark in a Lotus 30

Monaco but had taken the lap record at 1 min 43·6 sec. So even on the fastest British circuit the Monacos had the legs of the classic sports-racers, but the Lotus 15 was still a challenge, and more so with the 2½-litre FPF.

Le Mans 1959 saw another confrontation between the two, but the Lotus had transmission problems and retired, having run faster than the Cooper, which Russell crashed in the fifth hour in ninth position. At the Aintree British GP meeting, Keele Engineering had a 2½-litre Monaco for Moss on one end of the front row, Brabham's 2-litre in the middle and Hill's 2½-litre Lotus on the other side; in the event Moss had starting problems but took fastest lap, and victory went to Hill from Stacey (Lotus 2-litre) and Brabham (after a spin), followed by three Lister-Jaguars headed by Jim Clark.

So by mid-1959 it was established that small and light was beautiful and big front-engined cars were only good for long distance events where speed *and* reliability counted; however which end the engine went for sports cars was still not proven. The following year changed all that when Salvadori's later car had a 2½-litre Climax and that car won most of the season.

At the 1960 British GP Coopers made up a large proportion of the grid for the sports cars; Flockhart won in the Coombs car, Tom Dickson in the Ecosse Monaco ran second but retired, so Graham was second in a Lotus 15 2-litre from the remarkable Peter Ashdown in the Lola Mk.I 1100 and George Pitt's Cooper Monaco; others there included Tony Marsh, Escott, Osbiston and Brian Naylor's Ferrari-powered version. One car that should have been there, though, was the Lotus 19 but it wasn't ready—that was to come.

Although the Lotus 19 had an outing abroad at the end of 1960 it wasn't until 1961 that their dominance became immediately apparent and the three UDT-Laystall cars clocked several 1, 2, 3 at the decreasing number of big sports car races; Moss' time of 1 min 39 sec at the International Trophy Silverstone was a good 3 sec faster than a Monaco had managed.

Thus over a very short space of time the Monaco had been outclassed in that form, but by then the

FIA sports-car championship was for GT cars, so interest in two-seater racing cars in Europe declined. America though was different; Cooper Monacos and Lotus 19s were rapidly shipped over to take part in the forerunners of CanAm racing alongside Maserati Birdcages, Scarabs and Chaparral.

Among those competitors was one Roger Penske who had beaten Bruce McLaren's Cooper Monaco in a sports version of a 1960 GP Cooper. Eventually McLaren acquired this Zerex Special, then inserted a Traco-tuned Buick alloy V-8 and the McLaren CanAm cars were born.

However even in 1962 John Cooper was still developing the Monaco, and *Autocar* recorded that the brand new 1963 version, fitted with a 2·75-litre Climax was being shipped to the US, using the new Cooper five-speed box with current F1 suspension on a stronger chassis; the body showed a more pronounced nose and intake slots each side of the grille for larger front brakes. The box was presumably that developed by Cooper and Maddocks for the latter 2½-litre GP cars.

But the Climax in that form was somewhat fragile and it was natural for the Americans to use V-8s instead, both in Lotus 19s and Cooper Monacos. The 'King Cobra' followed with the 4·7-litre Ford in the latest Monaco and John Cooper recalls in his book that 25 were ordered by Carroll Shelby, so the car that turned European sports car racing round went on to sire the new generation of American sports car events, along with Lotus—although the Lotus 30/40 was never a success, the 19 was—and Lola.

Repeating history, our historic racing has seen first Maserati Birdcage and then Listers at the forefront of sports car classes, until the early 1980s when finally John Harper's red car recaptured the form that the marque showed in 1959.

Suddenly, as in 1959, the front-engined big sports-racers are facing the threat of demotion; however Listers are now faster than ever, but a good Cooper Monaco has already shown its mettle as and when the gearbox has allowed—2½-litres of 240 bhp FPF with modern historic tyres is really too much for a box whose origins stem from a 55 bhp Light Fifteen Citroen!

Porsche 906

We were driving gently round the Isle of Man TT course pondering the old question of which would be fastest around such a demanding course, car or motor cycle; at that time, 1967, the island fathers — or Tourist Board — were thinking seriously of arranging the ultimate confrontation. To be fair to two wheels and four we had to have two motor cyclists who knew the island well; that meant John Surtees and Mike Hailwood — that much was easy, and we felt pretty sure that John wouldn't insist on 37 miles of Armco!

Then we needed to choose the weapons; a road course demands a road car, an ultimate road car maybe, but a 50-off group 4 Sports car seemed the right level. What more logical than to choose the winner of the previous year's Targa Florio, on a circuit of similar character — a Porsche Carrera 6. Memory doesn't recall the equivalent motor cycle and, unfortunately, nothing came of the idea, but it was interesting that we both chose the Porsche 906 rather than the group 4 GT40 or Ferrari LM.

The mind's eye was picturing a little white speck down in the valley, that curiously sonorous baying howl echoing distantly; gradually the car would come nearer climbing the narrow hills fast, swinging through the bends; into sight and the low nose, high wheel arches with their inset rectangular headlamp surrounds, driver on the left, and louvred rear screen would be details just caught as the car disappeared in a blast of warm sound emanating from a pair of megaphones beneath the Kamm-like tail. The 906 had the right mixture of power and roadholding to stay on the road without sliding; on the Targa Florio balance is more important than sheer power, and even in later years Porsche would use the less powerful 908s instead of the 917s at both the Madonie and the Nürburgring.

Driving a 906 some 13 years later it still struck me as a Targa car. With its gull-wing doors it is quite easy to get into, stepping over the wide sill; bits of tubular frame are visible around you, under the scuttle and on the floor. Looking forward through

In drag terms, the shape of the 906 was not as good as the 904, but its stability was better. This was the first design of the Piech period at Porsche

the steeply raked panoramic screen, you find the wheel arches pretty prominent, which is good for aiming, and the fall-away centre gives a good view of the road from only just in front of the car. Behind, you can see little through that moulded coloured perspex screen via an inside mirror, the wing mirrors that most seemed to wear in their day really were needed.

I was trying No. 109 which had just been restored, and it was still fitted with very high gear ratios. At slow speed, getting the feel of it, the engine and gearbox had just the same nasal sound as a road-going 911 pulling at low revs. But once over 5000 rpm the car took on a new lease of life, leaping away with an almost 'big-engined feel'—with 220 bhp in about 1460 lb that isn't surprising, but the high specific output means that you have to wait for things to start.

On the road the tyres nibble at raised surfaces in a straight line so that the car feels a bit twitchy, but wind it into a corner and the tyres bite with an almost instant response, the steering informative of slight understeer. The car feels all of a piece, no rattles, just a mechanical glove built around you; it feels as if it could be chucked into a corner and balanced, rather than driven in and powered out. I'd like to have done more laps to find out but there wasn't time, but I had done enough to realise that back in 1967 the 906 was as good a choice as any for tackling that TT course.

To understand the 906 you have to look back to the 904. Porsche had been winning the 2-litre category of the GT championship in 1961-62 with the Abarth-Carreras, and they had amassed a lot of useful racing experience in all categories, including Formula 1 and the out-and-out mid-engined sports-racing RS series. So with the threat of serious opposition in the category from Abarth-Simcas and Alfa TZs, the men of Porsche conceived the 904, styled by Ferdinand Porsche III. Since the homologation requirement was for 100 cars in a year and Porsche wanted the car homologated in about four months of production, the 904 had to be designed almost as a production-line racer, based on the 1961 Le Mans coupes. The chassis itself looked almost vintage, a pair of boxed channels running fore-and-aft with underslung cross members, but the suspension was modern with twin wishbones, coil springs and telescopic dampers. Although the chassis didn't look particularly stiff it wasn't too flexible, and the idea was to increase it considerably

Gullwing doors give good access. Space frame tubes are visible in the workmanlike cockpit

Almost a standard 1960s design, but a Porsche giveaway is the air-cooled flat six

by bonding the glassfibre body to it; Porsche managed to contract out the whole assembly of chassis and body to Heinkel.

The original plan was to use the 904 as the test-bed for the 901 flat-six engine (subsequently 911), but that wasn't far enough advanced at the time and the four-cam flat-four Carrera '2' 2-litre was used as a basis, further developed to give 180 bhp at 7200 rpm or 155 bhp with road-going silencing. The engine was mounted ahead of the rear axle line with a new transaxle behind it. The fuel tank was set in the scuttle, which meant a change in weight distribution from full to empty, and the reservoir for the dry sump oil system was just behind the bulkhead.

It took most of 1963 to get the design finalised and production set up, but between November 1963 and April 1964 the required 100 were produced, of which ten were retained by the works. So their first works outing at Sebring saw them run as prototypes with the best placing ninth. They celebrated homologation by winning the Targa

101

Florio outright and by the end of the season had clocked another 2-litre GT championship; the same happened in 1965 which also included Bohringer's dramatic second overall in the Monte Carlo Rally.

Meanwhile during 1964 Porsche engineers were using flat-8 and flat-6 engines in 904s and running them in the prototype category, while hill-climb Spyders were also built, with extra tubes making up for the loss of the body reinforcement. They might have built a second batch of 904s with the six-cylinder, but with the reduction of the GT requirement to 50 cars for 1966, a new car was felt necessary, the Carrera 6. Part of the reason for the rejection of the 904 rather than its further development was the rise of the other half of the Porsche family; children of the original Ferdinand were Ferry and Louisa; Louisa married Anton Piech and had four children—the eldest Ernst married into the Nordhoffs of Volkswagen fame—while Ferry also produced four children. While it was Ferdinand Porsche III who masterminded the 904, it was his cousin Ferdinand Piech who was to have such an influence over the next generation of racing machinery of which the 906 was just a start.

Although the 906 was developed from the 904 the actual reversion to a space frame came via an instant replacement for the 904/8 hill-climb Spyder. As the Ferrari Dino was doing too well, Porsche needed a new hill-climb car in mid-1965; acquiring some Lotus hubs and uprights to allow 13-in wheels they quickly built up a space-frame with some 904 components. It didn't win, but paved the way for the 50-off 906.

The new car was designed to take the suspension system of the 904 which had been over-ordered against the possibility of that second batch—it was mounted on spherical joints this time; the wheelbase stayed the same too, but the track was widened largely as a function of wider wheels—7-in front and 9-in rear. It was a complex space frame running up to window level in the engine bay but dropping down to the sills for the gull-wing doors which were suspended from hoops fore and aft of the cockpit. Additional strength had to be obtained across the engine bay by a removable tube, while fuel tanks were hung in the sills. Against the 904/6 coupe the 906 was as stiff but considerably lighter. Like the 904, frame construction was contracted out to a local body-builder with the added problem of providing pressure-tight welds, as two of the tubes were required to carry oil to the cooler set in the upper part of the bonnet. Glassfibre body panels too were contracted out, and as these did not provide any stiffness they were as thin as possible; the aluminium sills were the fuel tanks.

Sleek though it was, the 906 was actually not as low in overall drag as the 904, being bigger in frontal area and inferior in drag factor, and the car soon earned a tail spoiler and nose trim-tabs, but its high speed stability was better than that of the 904.

Outwardly the 906 was powered by a 911 developed to produce some 220 bhp instead of the 130 bhp production tune. It was also considerably lighter by the use of magnesium castings instead of aluminium, although the heads remained in

Silumin while the cylinders used aluminium with a hard-chromed bore. Following its use in the GP engine, titanium was used for connecting rods and bolts as well as the main head clamping bolts. The forged crankshaft came from the 911 engine as did its bearings and the dry sump oil pumps.

In the heads a second plug was added, valve sizes were considerably increased and they were sodium filled, cams were wilder—single cam per bank with rockers to vee-disposed valves—and a pair of Weber triple-choke 46IDA3C instruments provided the carburation. The result was a minimum of 210 bhp at 8000 rpm from the 2-litre engine and this was mated to a version of the road-going 911 transmission with a wide variety of ratios.

By the end of 1965 the new car was ready for testing, clocking 1366 lb less fuel, or 180 lb less than the 904. The inaugural outing for a single car was the Daytona 24-hours in February 1966 and the prototype finished sixth behind four Mk. II Fords and a Ferrari. At the next round two works cars were joined by three privateers against a sole Dino; although the Ferrari led all the 906s for some time, it developed problems and the Hermann/Mitter/Buzetta works car took fourth. After this the 906s were strengthened somewhat with chassis gusseting and increase of some tube thicknesses, while brakes also received more cooling and quick-change calipers. Still running as prototypes the 906s beat the Dinos comfortably on their home ground at Monza taking 2, 3, 4 and 6 places with Dinos fifth and seventh.

Homologation came up at the beginning of May and the 906 won the Targa Florio outright; that was the start of a sports-car supremacy in their class that was to last them through to 1968. Meanwhile Bosch fuel injection had been fitted to some of the 906s to make them 906Es running in the prototype category; it wasn't very successful for them at the Nürburgring where two Dinos finished ahead, but at Le Mans, where the cars ran with special long noses and long tails, they finished fourth, fifth and sixth behind the three Fords. By the end of the season Porsche had won the 2-litre category in both prototypes and GT championships.

Some of the 906s had been equipped with 2·2-litre flat-8s giving 250 bhp and hope of outright victory on faster circuits, but that was not to be, as promising runs at the Targa Florio and the Nürburgring were spoilt by chassis breakages, a fact which prompted Porsche to try and ensure that all major races were started with new cars, the old ones being sold off to private entrants.

Just to clear up the chronology of the other 900-series cars, the 910 followed the 906 with some inspiration from the 1965 hill-climb car. The frame was similar to that of the 906 but stiffened by bonding the glassfibre panels to some of the tubing. Suspension was chosen to take 13-in wheels on wider rims than before and followed racing design of the time. The 910 appeared in 6 and 8-cylinder (2·2-litre) forms in 1966 and 1967, winning both the Targa Florio (910/8) and the Nürburgring 1000 Km (910/6). Since Porsche were selling off the 910/6s after racing them, production numbers gradually

built up and when the FIA announced that the GT production quantity would be reduced to 25, the 910/6 was suddenly a group 4 sports car. Came the 907 for 1967 long-distance racing as a 910 with smaller frontal area and lower drag factor in its 907L form for Le Mans and similar races, including the 1968 Daytona where three 907Ls took the first three places; that year saw the short-tail 907s using 2·2-litre flat-8s with victory again in the Targa Florio and at Sebring.

Hill-climbing was still a Porsche preoccupation and a pair of novel 909s were built in mid-1968; these anticipated the 908/3 by mounting the gearbox ahead of the transaxle, pushing the driver very far forward, to give a low polar moment car that was well suited to hill-climbing. And the 908 helped by the 907 was the car that took Porsche into their first world championship of makes in 1968 using a 3-litre flat-8, effectively a twin-cam version of the 911 with two more cylinders.

Throughout the five years from 1964-68 Porsche were developing racing sports cars at an almost incredible rate; the next one was on the drawing board before the previous one had won its first race. So the Carrera 906 was just a brief chapter in the Porsche racing book, from 904 through to the 917.

Despite the Carrera name, the Porsche 906 was totally suited to twisting circuits like the Nürburgring and the Targa Florio, winning outright in Sicily

Maserati Tipo 65

The big 5-litre Maserati V-8 looks impressive, but the engine area is almost dwarfed by the gearbox, with all the pipework for no fewer than four oil coolers

Big, red with a battery of stripes running from its rounded nose to its Kamm-shaped tail the Tipo 65 looked an impressive, even fearsome beast when I came to try it at Silverstone; it is no less impressive when you lift the tail. The 5-litre V-8 unit is big enough, but the five-speed transmission is massive; across its rear are no fewer than four engine oil coolers fed by ducts in the after deck. The coolers were originally plumbed in series but they now operate as pairs in parallel before returning to the dry sump reservoir. Fuel injection nestles in the bank of the vee while exhaust pipes curl up from the underside of the twin-cam heads to exit centrally. Since its period days it has grown trim tabs each side of the front radiator intake, which doubtless go some way towards controlling front end lift.

You sit well down in the cockpit with a good view forward over a low bonnet line. Behind, you have to rely on the mirror even for reversing. On your right is the gate for the five-speed box with the fifth forward and right opposite reverse. Ahead among sundry gauges and switches is the central 10,000 rpm rev-counter; in its 151 form with a wet-sump 5000 GT engine and Lucas fuel injection it has developed 430 bhp at 7000 rpm but 6000 rpm was all I was using after its rebuild. On the move the engine certainly felt touring-derived after rather spluttery pulling below 3500 rpm; beyond that, it was just smooth and powerful with no great kick in the back, just a steady shove with a subdued bark.

Brakes seemed to start soggy and get better as they warmed up; they were certainly well capable of pulling up nearly a ton with no effort. The car was running on M-section Dunlop racers— 6.00M × 15-in on 6½-in rims at the front and 6.50M × 15-in on 8-in rims at the back. In a straight line it felt quite stable with no wandering under braking; into a corner, you could feel initial understeer, but as you neared the exit it would change to oversteer, which always seemed to be lurking like a poised pendulum; in fact, it was quite catchable and you could exit under opposite lock power, but it didn't encourage one to enter a corner too quickly.

It wasn't until I was aware of it lurching back onto an even keel half way through Becketts when the oversteer took over, and later watching it come out of Woodcote and not lose its roll angle until the Motor bridge, that I realised that half its oddity was due to overly soft springs, particularly at the rear, with very firm dampers trying to cope; eventually it gets to the limit of suspension travel and you have instant oversteer.

It could certainly do with a lot more roll stiffness at both ends, preferably spring stiffness, to cut out attitude changes under braking and acceleration. As it was the left-hand front tyre just stayed cold and the hottest was the left-hand rear, which isn't right. But the solid rattle-free way it felt, its delightful gearbox (despite two fourths), its smooth powerful engine and its whole appeal suggest that the effort of adjusting its suspension would be thoroughly worthwhile and it would be a very rewarding car to drive. It actually felt quite a comfortable car for a 24-hour race but the handling would have made it pretty tiring; I suspect it is unlikely that such things as spring rates would have been changed since 1965, so I can understand how Siffert must have felt with the prospect of 24 hours racing ahead of him. At Modena, miracles are obviously possible but tuning takes a little longer.

However you look at it, the Maserati Tipo 65 was a disaster, albeit fortunately only a one-off disaster. But the man who bore the brunt of it was Colonel John Simone. Joel Finn's Maserati book quotes the sum invested by Simone as over £100, 000 and the work involved as 'up to thirty mechanics working day and night on the project' with work starting ten weeks before Le Mans 1965. If you assume that that means an average 20 men doing 15 hours a day for 70 days, the hourly rate works out at £5, which is at least of the right order. So Simone's investment certainly covered the majority of the costs in building Maserati's final fling in the sports-racing world, and the gradual rundown of the Maserati factory cannot really be blamed on the Tipo 65. But it was certainly a disaster for Simone as the car was shunted irretrievably on the first lap of Le Mans 1965.

Maserati had a relatively successful period with the front-engined Birdcage Tipos 60 and 61, in that the cars were fast if fragile, but they did win races. The 3-litre Tipo 61s continued into 1961 by which time the mid-engined Tipo 63 had joined the fray; this was really a converted Tipo 61 using the same front end and mating the 3-litre 'four' direct to that car's transaxle with wishbone suspension all round.

Continuing a policy of letting the privateers do the racing, Maserati produced four of these for Cunningham, Camoradi (Lucky Casner's team) and Scuderia Serenissima (Count Volpi's team) who had two; the two American ones competed at Sebring in 1961 but both retired although they had shown some speed despite suspect handling. The two Serenissima ones finished fourth and fifth in the

The cockpit of the Maserati Tipo 65 was quite comfortable, but its handling was somewhat less so

Targa Florio, but gave best to the Tipo 61 in a wet Nürburgring. Le Mans 1961 saw three of the mid-engined Tipo 63s powered by various versions of the short-lived V-12 which had been seen in a 250F and a 300S; the Cunningham version managed a fourth place, but the other two retired, one with brake failure after wrongly-fitted pads.

By the end of that season for the last event at Pescara one of the Serenissima cars had a 'birdcage' de Dion structure, but it wasn't to finish so the final showing saw Maserati second again in the sports car championship. Tipo 64 was the development of that car for the 1962 season still using the V-12, but no success was achieved.

That de Dion structure was the most complex looking device imaginable, and was apparently created to give additional roll stiffness while still retaining a de Dion axle. The hub carriers were located by fore and aft radius rods and extended rearwards to contain pivot points for a massive tubular structure which served as the bridge piece for the de Dion axle; this bridge wrapped around the end of the hub carrier extensions and was pinned to them to allow relative movement, which was constrained by horizontal coil springs between bridge and a drop arm from the hub carrier. Lateral location was provided by a sliding peg in the rear of the axle casing. Meanwhile the vehicle springing at that end was by longitudinal torsion bars, while amongst this maze of small diameter tubing there was also an anti-roll bar; dampers were attached to the hub carriers. If it actually functioned as intended I would be very surprised; as the car's handling was poor, perhaps it didn't.

Fortunately the system had been simplified a good deal by the time Maserati produced their new car for the 1962 Le Mans. This reverted to a front

engine layout in a brutal looking coupe; the rules allowed 4-litre GT prototypes so the engine used was a reduced version of the 450S V-8 and was coupled to a 450S transaxle. The chassis this time was more tubular than 'birdcage' but there were still a lot of small tubes around. Front suspension used conventional wishbones but the articulated de Dion axle now used a single-tube bridge piece; springing was by coil springs. Three of these new cars were built during the 1961-2 winter, two for Briggs Cunningham and one for the French Maserati distributor, Colonel John Simone. These three were entered for Le Mans and proved very fast in practice with the quickest achieving 177 mph down the straight, but all were involved in accidents while running near the front. There had apparently been an 'axle wind-up problem' in testing which was presumably due to excessive squat under acceleration as it was magnified with more powerful engines which Alfred Momo inserted into one of the Cunningham cars—first a 5·7-litre Maserati V-8 and then a 7-litre Ford. With the latter it also produced rear end steering, which contributed to its accident at Daytona on the banking when Marvin Panch—a stock-car racer—flipped it, but emerged unhurt.

Meanwhile the French car was rebuilt as a 151/1 the next winter with a production 4·9-litre V-8 allowed by new regulations; the incredible de Dion axle was replaced by a more normal tube arrangement and the shape reworked. This time at Le Mans it led for two hours before retiring with a failed final drive in the hands of Casner/Simon. With a new body and chassis with yet more changes Casner/Trintignant tried again in 1964; although it clocked 191 mph on the straight and eventually worked up to third place after four hours—a first lap stop to

Maserati Tipo 65 showing more roll than it should. It was an expensive failure for Colonel Simone

sort out throttle trouble delayed it—it retired after brake troubles and finally a flat battery. The Colonel decided to have another go for 1965 with further revisions of the Tipo 151 but at the Le Mans practice week-end Casner had a major accident under braking at the end of the Mulsanne straight and was killed.

While Simone was still using the 151 he was reluctant to invest in Alfieri's latest development on the Tipo 64 theme, but, with the death of Casner and the destruction of the Tipo 151, interest was quickly rekindled. Alfieri promised to produce the car in time for Le Mans. With Casner's death on April 10 and Le Mans on June 19 there wasn't much time in between, but they made it and the Tipo 65 was born.

The design reverted to the 'birdcage' theme and was bred from experience on the Tipos 63/64 and from the 151 whose 5-litre engine was used mated to a transmission which had the clutch at the rear. The de Dion was disposed of in favour of conventional wishbones of the trailing arm/ transverse link variety, while the front suspension used conventional wishbones. This was encased in a body which had origins in the Tipo 151 but with an open cockpit and a high tail on the same level as the top of the windscreen.

After the 10-week miracle which included testing at Modena the car arrived at Le Mans on schedule for Jo Siffert and Jochen Neerpasch; although both were quick in practice neither liked the car as its nose was lifting on the straight. Twenty-four hours of that was going to be hard work, but the car didn't even last a lap as Siffert hit a bank during the first lap scramble, breaking the radiator which lost fluid and that couldn't be replaced so early in the race. According to Joel Finn, the car came out again at the Rheims 12-hour race with a new nose but retired with fuel injection problems, but neither *Motor* nor *Autocar* commented on its performance or even appearance, so it can't have been very impressive.

That was enough for the Orsis who were disinclined to have any further works involvement in racing, although they were by then supplying Cooper with V-12 Maserati engines for Grand Prix racing. However the car was further modified at Maserati during 1966 but then passed to the Austrian, von Pumbhofer, who tried the car on several occasions but doesn't seem to have raced it.

From the Jo Siffert collection it came into the hands of Historic Sports Car Club Competition Secretary Bob Owen in 1973; after a year's work it emerged but Bob was never really happy with it; he let Willie Green have one spectacular outing which showed that the car could be driven quickly if you like driving like that—lurid opposite lock. Owen continued to use it occasionally in HSCC events, including also a major stint in the relay races, but finally sold it to Sid Colberg of Anglo-American Automobile Investments whose English end had just finished getting it running when I had a brief outing at Silverstone.

At Le Mans in 1962 the Tipo 151 ran with a reduced 450 engine but Trintignant and Bianchi retired with suspension failure after nine hours, when they were in seventh place. The third-placed Ferrari GTO follows

Ford GTs, and Mirages

The GT40 was still going strong in 1969, winning Le Mans that year when all the Porsche 917s had retired and Ickx had his 3-hour battle with a 908

Mention Ford GT40 and the memories come flooding back, staccato visions of sights seen and cars driven—Eric Broadley's hip-high Lola GT at the 1963 Racing Car Show, first Le Mans victory for the Mk. II in 1966, three very bent GTs (a Mk. IV and two Mk. IIBs) just over the hill into the Le Mans Esses at dawn 1967, teams and privateers at Rheims and the Nürburgring and Le Mans, the incredible three-hour dice to the end of Le Mans 1969 by GT40 and Porsche 908, and then my own drives—a few laps round Mallory Park in the Ford (UK) car, laps round the Ford Dearborn test track when

visiting Roy Lunn at Kar Kraft (the US research and building centre for the American teams), ten days of commuting in a GT40, a road run in von Karajan's Mk. III, track-testing a Mirage M1 and finally a run round a twisty private track in the JCB Mk. IV.

Somehow I missed a Mk. II, but I've probably driven more different Ford GTs than any other model in this book for the simple reason that it is such an appealing car that you never turn down the chance to drive one: easy effortless high performance, roadholding that is virtually unexploitable on the public roads, forgiving and controllable

The Mirage M1 had a narrower 'cabin' than the GT40 and lighter structure, but lacked reliability with the bigger engines

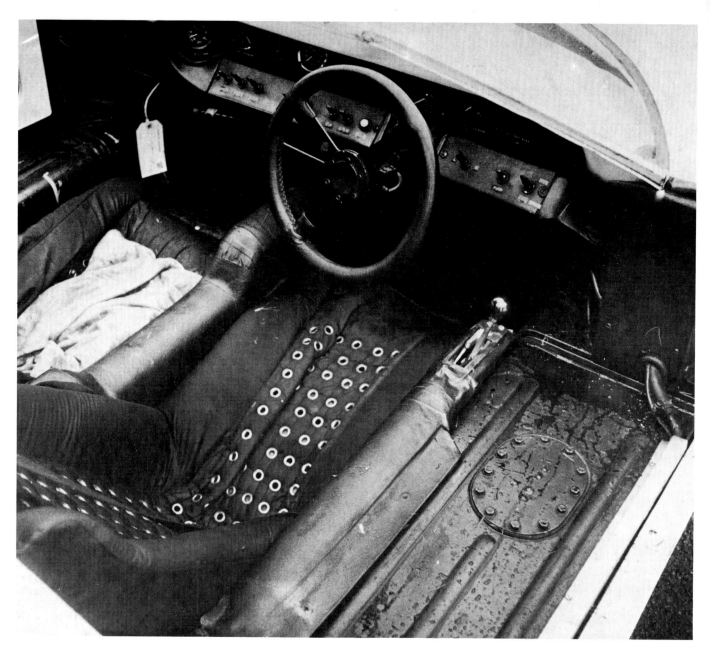

The neat and comfortable cockpit of the Mirage M1 is virtually identical to that of the GT40

handling, an excellent ride even on racing tyres on the road, and its whole feel of one-ness, made and make it a quite exceptional overall design, a triumph, for once, of computer over man.

Hip-high the GT40 certainly was, as the '40' was supposed to refer to its overall height in inches; its big doors look like gull-wings as they are set well-into the roof-line abutting the central bracing strip, but they are front-hinged and the car is reasonably easy to get into. Stepping over the high fuel-containing boxed sills, one foot goes straight to the floor and, as you sit down, you bring the other leg over, carefully avoiding the right-hand gear lever which is prone to vanishing up your trouser leg. If you prefer to lean against the seat back-rest and slither down be careful that a wind isn't blowing — the doors are reminiscent of a horizontal guillotine!

For a racer, the GT40 is incredibly well-trimmed and equipped. The seat is a comfortable hammock with the pedals adjustable in a sliding pedal-box; the facia contains a full complement of instruments for every function as well as eye-ball fresh-air vents —

there's even a speedometer, although that is for the passenger only. It was certainly designed to be a comfortable long-distance racer with a good view out over the front 180 degrees; you can see the tops of wheel arches and some of the bonnet with only another two-and-a-half feet unseen. Behind you is a bit of a mystery: the rear quarters are covered in bodywork and the interior mirror view has to penetrate one vertical piece of glass, pass across the top of the carburettor intakes and out through angled perspex — alright when everything is clean but difficult in bad weather or when there are headlights behind you.

Starting the engine only requires the standard two or three squirts on the throttle for the Webers and the 4·7-litre Ford V-8 bursts into life just behind you, noisy urgent life with a deep throaty bark as revs rise and fall quickly with throttle blips, and you can hear the trumpets gulping for air. On the track cars the handbrake was a primitive affair, leaning directly on to the brake pedal, which was very effective, if scarcely street-legal. On the right, the gear lever is a delight; you sit reclining in the hammock with your feet on the adjustable pedals, the steering wheel is comfortably placed just above the thighs with your arms almost straight, and the lever sits just where your hand drops naturally onto the sill. It has a sequential gate, which means that the lever has to visit every slot on the way up or down the box or you can't engage the gear—it can be confusing if you have coasted to a halt in third or fourth because you won't get first until you have gone via second, but in general use it gives a superb slicing action, which feels just like purely fore-and-aft movement with slight sideways pressure according to the desire for higher or lower gears.

With pedals ideally spaced for heel-and-toe use, gearchanging is its own satisfaction; it doesn't matter that the ZF synchromesh is very powerful on all gears—the heel and toe tap-dance with a raucous response is music to the senses.

Away from rest it isn't fantastically fast—its 300 bhp/ton plus is no more than for a Lister–Jaguar and its acceleration times similar—but it just keeps on accelerating with splendid torque over a 2500-6000 rpm range, and it is still accelerating above 140 mph where open cars are beginning to meet nature's brick wall. Stopping power is very much that of a giant hand; the brakes haul the car down to saner speeds with a complete lack of drama with no nose-diving pitch—wide tyres might nibble on surface ridges, but road-width rubber is un-temperamental.

For a racing car on the road the ride is amazingly good; spherical joints all round might generate rattles, but the car is so taut that even frost-damaged surfaces can be taken surprisingly quickly with only little tugs on the steering wheel, and tyre thumps as a minimal reaction. Out on the open road or track, the ride is that firm well-damped feel of perfect suspension which seems to generate no roll—masked anyway by good seats—and it swallows humps and hollows without ever reaching the ends of its suspension travel; even a slight airborne moment on a rapid bridge produced no bottoming.

Standard GT40 wheel sizes became 6- and 9-in rims on 15-in wheels, while road-going Mk. IIIs seemed to use 5½/8J on front/rear, but developed racing GT40s and the Mirage M1 were considerably wider to take 9.20/12.00 tyres, or near enough, depending on whose racing tyres you were using. Thus comments on the ultimate roadholding inevitably vary according to the tyre width from remarkable to very good indeed for racing use in their day. Most of the previous comments have been applicable to almost any GT40, but the road-going Mk. III is very much more civilised without apparently losing any of the track-type response although, doubtless, a track test would have revealed the differences more noticeably.

To start with the Mk. III used considerably softer spring and damper settings; then the nose was modified to take four headlights behind perspex covers and at a legal height, while the tail was

Mirage M1 was a modified GT40 running in the prototype category with Ford engines up to 5·7 litres; it is seen here at a Thruxton historic race

modified to clear a flat insulated case for little more than overnight 'grips'; the exhaust system runs underneath this rather than emerging above the top of the gearbox, and the gear lever is centrally mounted so the radiator water pipes are moved into the sills. In fact, 'my' ex-von Karajan car, built in 1968, used left-hand drive, so the lever was still right-handed with almost the same precision as those with outset levers.

A run in the ex-Andretti 1967 Sebring Mk. IV round a private test-track was more exhilarating in sheer performance than in sampling the ultimate road-holding; like the smaller versions, it was very comfortable but there was no real chance to see if the extra weight of the 7-litre adversely affected the handling. The Ford-built four-speed gearbox gave almost as good a change as the ZF although most of the time I was only using second and third.

Meanwhile John Wyer had been running smaller capacity GT40s, but these were obviously being outclassed by the Ford developed Mk. IIs and then Mk. IVs, so for 1967, JW Automotive evolved the Mirage M1. This conformed with prototype regulations and was effectively a lightened GT40 with modified roof (more tumblehome for lower frontal area) and a modified tail section to take wider wheels with either 5 or 5·7-litre versions of the small-block Ford. On a power-weight ratio it had a chance against the bigger Fords but in practice lacked reliability; however a victory at Spa 1967, plus non-championship wins at Karlskoga and Kyalami proved that the concept was sound before the championship rules allowed the GT40 to continue its life as a 50-off group 4 sports car. Understandably the Mirage feels just like a GT40 with the narrowed screen-top hardly intruding on passenger space or visibility.

The next Mirage stage was the M2 for 1969; this used a certain amount of Gulf Ford GT40 experience in a chassis designed by Len Terry to take the BRM V-12 engine, the theory being that a racing 3-litre lightweight was going to be faster than the ageing GT40, but by the time the M2 arrived, the sports-car production quantity had been reduced to 25, which enabled Ferrari and Porsche to come up with virtually racing 5-litre sports cars. All might not have been lost though, if the BRM had produced its promised power, but a mere 325 bhp against a claimed 375 bhp was a lot to lose; even with a Cosworth substitution, it only once showed potential in a championship race when Ickx led in Austria from a 917, although he later won a non-championship race at Imola in the open car that had become M3-01.

The continued raceworthiness of the GT40 undoubtedly hampered M2 development leading into 1969, and this was compounded by the fact that considerable tyre-width development took place in the time between its original concept at the end of 1967 and its racing in 1969.

Driving the M2 with a BRM two-valve V-12 was certainly fun and the engine feels very nice and smooth—an important anti-vibration feature against a Cosworth for long-distance racing—but it just wasn't very powerful and would be no match for a

The McLaren/Donohue Ford Mk. IV finished fourth at Le Mans in 1967 behind the winning Ford and two Ferrari P4s

GT40 on today's historic tracks. It had handling quirks in its day with a lively tail, but the only ones I could notice were associated with running on long obsolete Firestones.

Although not strictly associated with the Ford GT40, the M2 was effectively put into total eclipse by its own predecessor, which says a lot for that basic design.

Those who live on the UK side of the Atlantic firmly believe that Eric Broadley's Lola GT, which appeared at the Racing Car Show in January 1963, was the real progenitor of the GT40; as the Lola Mk. VI the car used a monocoque frame with glassfibre bodywork and carried the Ford 4·2-litre V-8 and a Colotti gearbox amidships. Meanwhile Ford in America had announced in mid-1962 that they were returning to motor sport, and would like to aim at victory in the Indianapolis 500 and the Le Mans 24-hour race as the ultimate in prestige wins, which could be commercially exploited.

While the top brass were discussing the take-over of Ferrari towards this end—and the 1960 Ferrari Dino which found its way to Chinetti had been scheduled as a present from Ferrari to the Ford Museum in 1962—engineers, under Englishman Roy Lunn, had been looking at their own way of achieving the results. To some extent the little mid-engined Mustang, powered by Ford V-4, comes into the concept part of the story as that too was built in 1962, but the only recognisable thought to emerge in the GT40 was the fixed-seat adjustable pedal set up.

Ford soon built a scale model to test lift and drag and a full-size mock-up to test cooling air paths for interior, engine and brakes, but by this time Broadley almost had a completed car, although it appeared in January with wooden springs! It was racing (unsuccessfully) at the Nürburgring in May 1963, when the Ford/Ferrari negotiations were public knowledge, and by mid-1963 Ford had decided to join forces with Eric Broadley. Ford immediately ordered two Lola GTs for evaluation in England and America and lured John Wyer from Aston Martin; by April 1964 the first two GT40s were on their way to the Le Mans test week-end.

Although the Ford computer had apparently been used to produce the Mk. II version of the AC Cobra chassis, it was used to far greater effect with the GT40. However there is little point in feeding and using a computer unless it has *all* the facts, and an unrigid chassis is like 'an undamped fifth spring of unknown magnitude' to quote Roy Lunn when I visited him during the Mk. IV period; so the GT40 tub is exceptionally strong, as longevity and crash-survival were to show. The basic structure was made up from 0·026 in. sheet steel with strength provided by fuel-cell-containing sills, a massive

No need for complicated carburettor set-ups when you have 7 litres of torque and unstressed power. The Ford Mk. IV used a Ford gearbox casing with Galaxie internals

boxed scuttle cum footwell area, and a rear diaphragm joined to the screen top and surround; arms extended from the sills inwards and backwards to carry the transverse rear suspension links, so that all suspension loads were fed into the stiff frame rather than into sub-frames bolted on. Steel was chosen for strength and rigidity, although the sills were as prone to rusting as any road car some ten years later! Even with the iron-block 4·7-litre, though, the cars apparently weighed in at a 1960 lb.

Suspension followed an established theme of double wishbones at the front, while the rear took the twin trailing arms per side from the rear bulkhead, with a single top link and an inverted lower wishbone. Brakes from Girling were outboard with sliding spline drive-shaft joints, later replaced by 'doughnuts' to cushion wind-up and ease locking under torque. Wheels initially were spoked Borranis and the Mk. III retained these, but racing cars were soon switched to a variety of alloy wheels.

While both Ford and Broadley chose a Colotti gearbox for its torque capacity and both used 4·2-litre engines, the Lola had to use a stock cast-iron block, while Ford were able to make use of their Indianapolis engine with aluminium block and

head and dry sump to produce around 350 bhp.

The first appearance was in April 1964 at the Le Mans test days but both cars crashed in the wet conditions due to poor aerodynamics; a tail spoiler and a bluffer front end improved things and the solo entry in the Nürburgring 1000 km ran in the top five for $2\frac{1}{2}$ hours until the rear suspension broke. At Le Mans none of the three cars finished although they ran well and Phil Hill took the fastest lap of the race; the Colotti gearbox was troublesome and it was to affect them at Rheims too.

Ford handed these cars over to Shelby-American at the end of 1964 for further development while they worked on the Mk. II; Shelby's team opted for the standard cast-iron block 4·7-litre that they had developed with the Cobras and tried to improve the four-speed box with Ford gears. Other changes took place in aerodynamics, internally for cooling and externally for stability, while the spoked wheels were replaced by $8/9\frac{1}{2}$-in rim alloy wheels. By mid-1965 the cars were judged to be sufficiently developed to start 50-off production for sports car homologation.

By now Ford were aware of the need for even more power to take them towards that elusive Le Mans victory and, with prototype regulations so

Full of promise, but lacking predicted power in its BR17 engine, the Mirage M2 was never a match for the GT40 it was designed to replace

Mirage M2-01 was renumbered M3-01 when modified to take the Cosworth DFV engine; at the Nürburgring Ickx and Oliver kept it in sixth place until vibrations loosened too many nuts

little restricted, they went for the biggest engine available, their 7-litre 427 cu in, cast-iron V-8 using aluminium heads and dry sump lubrication; it had masses of torque, and was an engine that Ford knew well from stock-car racing. This was mated to Ford's own transmission, a new casting with Galaxie innards, tried and tested.

Although fundamentally, a developed GT40, the Mk. II required a complete detail redesign, starting with the rear bulkhead and thus seating position; a bigger spare wheel and larger radiator dictated a new front, while just about every duct size was increased. The year 1965 started well for the GT40s, with victories at Sebring and Daytona, but Le Mans, where two of the 7-litres ran very fast, was a disaster—none of the four GT40s finished, suffering either engine or transmission failures.

Detail development of the Mk. II continued into

1966 and the year of success; victory at Daytona and Sebring, second at Monza and Spa, and then 1, 2, 3 at Le Mans gave them the championship, as well as that target of three years earlier.

Meanwhile work had been taking place on the J-car using a much lighter tub made from an aluminium-epoxy honeycomb sandwich; although it was striking it wasn't as fast as the Mk. II until it earned longer nose and tail sections, by which time it had become the Mk. IV for 1967, and Mk. IIs were similarly bodily developed into Mk. IIBs. However Ferrari were back in fighting form with the 330P4 and Ford lost the first round; they took Sebring and Le Mans once again, after which the rules were changed and the old faithful GT40 took on a new lease of life. Sheer brute power seemed to have had its day, but only two years later even more power was available.

Lola T70

Although the Lola T70GT can be called a GT40 development, it has always struck me as a considerably more fearsome projectile, something to be treated with much more respect than a good old GT40, which I have driven on road and track, wet or dry on a number of occasions. The Lola is lighter, faster and some four years on.

Once again, it was to be a wet track test although light rain had only just started when I climbed into Richard Bond's 1969 Lola T70 Mk. IIIB. It is very much standard sports-racer—a pair of seats between a pair of fuel tanks, heels on the stressed floor skin with lower front wishbones coming into the cockpit. This one, with a background of long-distance racing and road car, is rather more instrumented than most—there was even a speedometer which had some figures on it, but I never saw whether it worked!

It usually fires on the starter button, but little Varleys can get rather tired churning big Chevrolets on cold wet days, so three-man power was used instead. In second gear it soon fired with that ferocious roar of an F5000-type engine which is very audible inside too; you are well protected from the engine by the official bulkhead and there is a clear plastic window at the forward end of that viewing tunnel on the rear deck, but the exhaust is still very evident.

The reassuring thing about driving the car for the first time is that you can see some car ahead of you, like wheel arch tops and mirrors on them; on some overwedged cars like the LM Ferrari you see nothing beyond the screen and are very conscious that your legs are the nearest thing to the accident.

A big 5-litre engine with a 6000 rpm rev limit is still well blessed with useable torque from around 3500 rpm upwards, so it isn't too hard to keep it on the cam at gentle speeds. With about 550 bhp/ton on tap throttle response is instant and it is certainly very fast. It was a lap or two before I used full throttle in third on the straight; the big wet Goodyears took it all and shot the car forward as if it were on slicks and a dry track. The Hewland LG600 gearbox was as short and precise in its travel as a much smaller box and it was no trouble to flick through the five-speed gate, still feeling tremendous acceleration comfortably over 100 mph in fifth.

Once the rain started to come down, the big single wiper coped admirably and I'm pleased to say that the tyres were as effective at transmitting brake torques as tractive ones. It's obviously a little difficult to comment on handling after a few wet laps, particularly when that much excess power is bound to spell oversteer, but it is set up to start with a reassuring amount of understeer which can easily be felt through remarkably light steering—not the sort of understeer that you have to counteract by a hefty boot on the throttle. Throttle response is gradual

Although the T70 Mk. 3 Lola showed plenty of promise the model only achieved one international victory, at Daytona in 1969

enough to keep it balanced without it biting; on the few dry occasions he has had to experiment with, Richard has found the handling very nice and predictable and has yet to discover the full limit despite a Club lap time of 58·7 sec. What I found surprising about the car was that it felt so much smaller than it looked; it didn't really feel that much larger than the Chevron B16 (a similarly-shaped GT) I had driven five years before with a 1·8-litre FVC engine.

The Lola T70GT story started with the dramatic announcement of the Lola GT at that 1963 Racing Car Show; after a moderately successful showing at Le Mans where the car was up to eighth after 10 hours, the project merged with that of Ford Advanced Vehicles to produce the GT40 and Eric Broadley moved to Slough. Broadley has contributed a lot to racing car design over the years and it was nice to see that in 1975 they produced the thousandth Lola, having started with the little 1100 cc sports-racing Mk. I Lola-Climax in 1958. The document accompanying the announcement showed all the production numbers and depicted milestones of Lola progress; these included the 1963 Lola GT, the 1966 Indianapolis T90, the 1968 T70 Mk. IIIB, the 1971 CanAm T260 and the 1974 F5000 T330.

The T70 started as Lola's CanAm car for 1966 and John Surtees' victory in that championship set the demand pattern, particularly since Lola were actually producing T70s for sale; group 7 racing was also taking place in the UK at the time, which widened the market and 47 T70/T70 Mk. IIs were built in 1965-66. In 1967 the sports and GT regulations were vague and there was no limit on prototype engine capacity; adding a high speed body to the CanAm design for such racing would broaden the market further although Lola were to rely upon works-backed, as opposed to works, entries to spread the gospel.

Different regulations and the need for long-distance high speed reliability meant that the suspension was strengthened for the greater weight, although the actual chassis was substantially the same as that for the Mk. II, which could thus be made into a GT with the optional body. It was a

striking body design evolved in the wind tunnel, although it was to need fins and spoilers for really high-speed work. Lola's association with Specialised Mouldings was in evidence then as it had been with the Mk. I.

The chassis followed standard practice for limited production runs in using a central monocoque tub with side sponsons carrying the fuel and providing the rigidity. Broadley used his own cast uprights to carry conventional suspension systems; twin wishbones at the front followed Lola Mk. I practice with transverse forward links and leading rear ones to resist brake torques. At the rear the effective wide-angle wishbones used a single rather short top link, and an inverted wishbone controlling toe-in with parallel near-trailing radius arms; all pick-ups use length adjustable spherical joints.

The engine is cradled between the rear legs of the side sponsons to which a bridge is attached to support lugs on top of the final drive unit; this supports the rear of the engine with the Hewland gearbox slung behind.

Although it was announced with Chevrolet power—5·4-litre, 460 bhp—the works were to co-run the Lola-Aston with the then-new Aston V-8. The Lola-Aston's first appearance was at the 1967 Le Mans test-day when the car was third fastest. At the Nürburgring 1000 Km that year, a sole entry for Surtees/Hobbs retired after six laps with a broken rear wishbone when around seventh place after a poor start. Then came Le Mans and two entries for Surtees/Hobbs and Irwin/de Klerk; that was an expensive disaster which should have put Aston Martin off Le Mans for ever. A last minute change of plug manufacturer had the Surtees car blow a piston after three laps, while the other staggered around the back with gear linkage trouble until its engine expired.

The big GTs were now in many private hands and a fortnight after Le Mans, four cars ran at the Rheims 12 hour race; after four laps they occupied the first four places against quite an impressive array of Fords and Ferraris; but by the fourth hour one remained, the Hulme/Gardner Sid Taylor car in the lead, but that too retired.

Sadly that was rather the pattern of the Lola Mk. III; it lacked works development although

At the 1969 BOAC 500 Sid Taylor's Lola T70 Mk. 3B was driven by Revson, Axelsson and Hulme, but retired after losing a water pump drive belt

many were campaigned over the following four years, and none ever finished at Le Mans. For 1968 prototypes were limited to 3 litres and GTs to 5 litres with a minimum production of 50. By this time Lola had produced more than 50; it was homologated and ran with 5-litre engines in Mk. IIIB form with suspension and body revisions, dictated by aerodynamics and even wider tyres.

In 1968 no points were scored in International Championship meetings but in the lesser events the car did well—Guards Trophy Oulton first (Redman), TT first (Hulme), Martini Trophy first (Hulme), Guards Trophy Brands first (Gardner). For 1969 with the production requirement reduced to 25, cars like the Lola T70 became instantly obsolete in favour of the Porsche 917 and the Ferrari 512; but with the Penske/Sunoco team the T70 achieved probably its best result—first in the Daytona 24-hour race with a second and seventh as well. Bonnier's second in the Austrian race at the end of the season brought the tally to third in the championship behind Porsche and Ford (still with the GT40). In home and lesser foreign events the car was very successful in the hands of private owners; Silverstone 30 March 1, 2, 3 with Hulme, Redman and Hawkins; Guards Trophy Snetterton 1, 2 with Hawkins and Bonnier; Thruxton 7 April 1, 2, 3 with Redman, Bonnier and Hawkins; Montlhéry first (Piper); Magny Cours 2, 3 with Hawkins and Piper; Martini Trophy 1, 2, 3 for Craft, Redman and Piper; a 1, 2 at the TT for Taylor and Piper; a win at Montlhéry again for Bonnier and finally a win at Nurnberg for Redman. That year had shown the car's fine ability in the shorter races but it always lacked stamina, a problem that was to afflict the similarly-engined F5000 cars; the T70 had also demonstrated considerable strength as those who saw Jo Bonnier's cartwheeling exercise at the BOAC 1000 Km will remember.

By then, though, regulations had killed off the T70 and Lola weren't in a position to take on the might of Porsche and Ferrari with their 25-off prototypes, so the lessons learnt by Broadley and his team were transferred to the F5000 T150 and the CanAm T160.

This particular car, chassis No L76/148, was completed on 12 March, 1969 as one of the last Mk. IIIB—the final number was 153. It was sold to Picko Troberg via Jo Bonnier with a 304 cu in Chevrolet engine. It went to the Nürburgring 1000 Km in June 1969 wearing the PR for Men colours but was reduced to a 'horrible heap against the bank' (my own words when covering that race for *Motor*) by Bjorn Rothstein. The next we hear of it is back at Lola in August 1969 being rebuilt, which took about six weeks, and it was then sold to Barrie Smith. He took it to the Buenos Aires race in January 1970 and hit a dog which necessitated borrowing a nose cone from Sid Taylor, but he didn't finish in the results.

I'm not sure whether it performed again in Europe that year, but Smith took it to the Kyalami 9-hours in November to drive with Jackie Pretorius but didn't figure in the results. It hadn't been too successful by this time and in 1971 it was sold to a Mr Farley, who converted it to a road car with some silencing and a more tractable state of tune and painted it blue. Mike Weatherill, who owned the Lotus 15 described elsewhere in this book acquired the car during 1974 but didn't use it. Richard Bond, well known for his regular finishes as a privateer at Le Mans, bought the car in October 1974.

By now it needed a complete rebuild which was undertaken by freelance race preparer Louis Lorenzini; the engine is basically a Traco F5000 unit with Alan Smith heads and develops around 440 reliable bhp. In five mostly wet races in 1975, Richard gained two firsts, a second plus a fifth and seventh with overheating problems.

Since then it has joined the Historic racing fray where it is a regular front-runner alongside another T70GT and a GT40 which uses the 5-litre Gurney-Weslake version of the Ford V-8—quite like old times; however, as in former days the T70 has the legs of the GT40 in short sprints, but not surprisingly both are liable to be beaten by the lighter CanAm equivalents.

The T70 wasn't a great car in GT form, but if Broadley had managed to retain his Ford association and take advantage of the Ford development work for long distance racing, it might have been—until the arrival of the Porsche 917s that is.

Porsche 917

Peering down that blue valley with blue hills rising each side and a parallelogram wiper flailing in front, I couldn't help but think back to that very wet BOAC 1000 Km at Brands Hatch in 1970 when Pedro Rodriguez drove at seemingly unabated speed through a continuous downpour to win in a Gulf-Porsche 917. The blue contours belonged to the front of a Gulf 917, one that Rodriguez drove to victory on at least two occasions, though not at that epic Brands Hatch; it was acquired by a consortium from the factory, who with scant respect for the past seemed to have little further use for it. I managed to catch it in private testing after a rebuild/overhaul by Classic Autos. Maybridge Engineering had tended to the engine.

Leaning well back in the seat you are very conscious of those two great wheel arches, although they look less conspicuous from the side since the whole car is very little higher than the wheel-arch tops. In front there are only a few ducts, the radiator intake and outlet—oil needs a lot of cooling on an air-cooled car—and your legs. The clutch is on the centreline, and has a substantial foot-rest alongside to act as counter-brace to high cornering forces. Steering wheel and right foot controls are better placed, with a smooth pro-gressive throttle with the long travel that makes such a powerful car remarkably easy to drive gently; it had to be, as this was another wet track test. In fact the 4·5-litre flat-12 is docile once started; it was happy to tick over at around 1200 rpm with an occasional spit-back, and even pull from 2000 rpm at which only the gearbox protested, with the typical nasal graunch of a Porsche box pulling at low revs. From 5000 rpm it all starts to happen with a tremendously powerful shove in the back towards the imposed red-line at 8000 rpm. On a wet track I only used 6500 rpm—peak torque and 520 bhp—which meant very short visits indeed to each slot of the five-speed gate; the right-hand lever uses the overdrive fifth pattern with a first gear detent as well, and has a nice smooth positive feel to it, with effective synchromesh.

With all that 580-odd bhp in 1790 lb and a wet

One of Pedro Rodriguez' great drives was his vic-tory in the 1970 BOAC 1000 Km in appalling conditions. That's a Ferrari on the right

track, I never used full throttle in second, but did in the three higher gears, reaching around 135 mph before the next braking point loomed uncomfortably quickly. Through the corners on part throttle the intakes would give occasional sharp spits, but always the flat-12 came on full song the moment the throttle was opened. Downchanges for tighter corners were a delight and the tail instantly responsive to too much throttle on the exit, although it certainly put a lot of the power down for very rapid acceleration.

Catching a tail that can be provoked that quickly on wet roads requires more practice than I am ever likely to achieve but, yes, it can be caught with high-geared and responsive steering; this was heavier than I expected but it heightened the effect of diminishing grip on the slippery bits—good feel. With really gripping seats and a six-strap harness you don't notice cornering forces until they get very high, but it certainly gripped well until it stepped bodily sideways on mid-corner puddles.

Although you are conscious of the wheel-arches in front of you the overall effect is of good visibility over somewhat more than 180 degrees; backwards, you use a mirror aiming across the intakes down the slot between the wedged halves of the afterbody. Without a centre aerofoil you would actually be aware that someone else was looming behind—as long as he too had a 917; with the aerofoil, well you can see some of the scenery some of the time.

I have driven fast cars slowly and sometimes quickly before, but none quite as potentially fast as this; it was uncanny how remote you felt from the smooth and not over-noisy engine. More revs didn't mean a lot more noise, and the vibration was minimal; it seemed as if the throttle pedal was connected to some external pushing device, quite unlike the normal effect of being directly in control of the power unit on board.

In view of the conditions I didn't return the 917 as reluctantly as I might have done, but it was a fascinating car—the last of the real sports-racers.

As an example of a car designed at great expense seemingly entirely to make a mockery of the CSI's good intentions, it is a classic in another sense. The year 1967 had seen the end of the unlimited capacity prototypes in which the power units were largely American with Ferrari's biggest at 4·4-litres. The Ford GT40 4·7-litre had become homologated as a 50-off sports car for 1966 and ran as such that year and in 1967 with little hope of outright victory, but with good chances for privateers in the sports category. Then for 1968 the sports-prototype capacity limit was dropped to 3-litres with 3 months' public notice and once again the GT40s were in with a chance with a top-limit of 5 litres— the rules still stated 50-off, dropping to 25 the following year.

The Lola T70s were also included although this was based on the assumption that the Mk. IIIGT was merely a CanAm car with an optional body, since 47 of the group 7 cars were built in 1965-66 and 25 of the group 4 Mk. IIIs in 1967. Lowering the production quantity required for group 4 cars to 25

for 1969 was only a detail change to the rules but one that made a major difference to Porsche whose 917 in coupe and CanAm forms, unblown and turbocharged, considerably enhanced their reputation all over the world.

Porsche had already started to develop the 908 for the 3-litre formula but weren't going to make 50 completely new cars of any type. However, the prospect of 5-litres wasn't beyond them and doubtless their pressure was added to the CSI; so mid-1968 saw the start of work on the 917. Previous work on the 908 was to prove useful; the aluminium-tube space frame was like that developed for the 908 with the cockpit further forward to clear the longer engine, while the flat-12 used the flat-8 bore and stroke dimensions; as with the H-16 BRM this allowed the use of already developed rods, pistons and general valve gear albeit at a narrower valve angle, but this development short cut was more successful; the greater torque meant a new gearbox which contained five speeds in its magnesium casing.

With 86 × 66 mm dimensions, the engine capacity at 4494 cc was smaller than allowed, but Porsche thought 580 bhp in just over 1760 lb was fast enough to cope with GT40s and Lolas on circuits where the greater agility of their 908s wasn't at a premium. Casings generally, including the vertically split crankcase, were of magnesium, while the heads and separate cylinders were in aluminium with chrome-plated bores. Twin camshafts per bank were gear-driven from the centre of the eight-bearing crankshaft, as was the output shaft running underneath the crankshaft with a 32/31 slight overdrive gearing. Two valves per cylinder was quite satisfactory. Fuel injection was by a Bosch mechanical system.

The complex space frame was welded up with the tubes interconnected so that an inflation pressure check could be made to detect cracks in the structure; this didn't of course include tubes carrying oil to the front radiator which are subject to their own pressure check nor the removable ones across the engine bay. When the 1971 regulations demanded stronger roll-hoops these were bolted in place around the engine bay to brackets welded to existing chassis; since these were not an essential part of the structure, they didn't need to be coupled into the pressure testing. Weight of the early chassis was a mere 103 lb.

Magnesium, titanium and aluminium were widely used in the chassis and running gear to keep the weights right down, with magnesium uprights and wheels and aluminium wheel nuts as examples. The body was made in glass fibre reinforced polyester with the parts that didn't need removing being bonded to the chassis. With high speed very much in mind for the fast circuits used in the sports car championships—Le Mans, Spa, Osterreichring, Daytona, Monza—the body first shown was very much a low-drag shape with stability controlled by added-on self-adjusting rear trim tabs. The drag factor for that was 0·33 but short tails with a 0·4 factor were also offered. The problem with any highly aerodynamic body shape is that the lift can

The air-cooled flat-12 has a very wide torque range and gives phenomenal acceleration; everything on it is designed down to the limit

The purely functional interior of the 917, with glassfibre floor bonded to tubes

change rapidly with attitude variation, so the trim tabs were connected to the rear suspension to try and keep the tail level, while the front suspension had 50 per cent anti-dive. All this was subsequently considerably modified, but the chassis remained more or less constant under a variety of interchangeable body-shapes covered broadly under the L and K suffixes for Lang and Kurt. The basic chassis change was the removal of the high degree of anti-dive to nearer 5 per cent to improve high speed stability. Suspension adjustments were mostly dictated by the use of ever wider tyres; the cars had been developed at Nürburgring where you need as much suspension travel as possible, so tyre sections were kept narrow on the same 9- and 12-in rims that the 908 used. This avoided excessive camber change effects. However, as the wheel rims were gradually increased to the 12- and 17-in widths the suspension was stiffened to limit the movement and consequent camber variations.

The 917 was first displayed to the public at the Geneva Motor Show in March 1969 and by April, 25 cars were shown complete to the CSI; they were offered to the public at about £14,500 although doubtless Porsche exercised some control over the buyers. The 1969 Spa 1000 Km was the first race entered, but a dropped valve in the first lap after a wet practice meant that little useful was learnt. A

The winning Gulf 917 at Daytona in 1971, where it was driven by Rodriguez and Oliver

single entry for David Piper/Frank Gardner at the Nürburgring 1000 Km was nursed to eighth place well down on the 908s, so by Le Mans development hadn't really proceeded apace. This was the year of the Hill/Rindt Barcelona wing failures when suspension controlled wings were instantly banned. However, after considerable discussion they were allowed on the 917s at Le Mans since the cars would have had to be withdrawn as they were undriveable at high speed without them. In the event the Rolph Stommelen/Kurt Ahrens long-tail car led for the first hour before it broke, then the Jo Siffert/Brian Redman 908 took over but when its transmission broke, the Vic Elford/Richard Attwood long-tail led until the bell-housing broke with 2½ hours to go. Then followed that epic dice when the Gulf GT40 just pipped the sole surviving 908 by two seconds. Sadly the only other 917, a short-tail driven by John Woolfe, crashed on the first lap killing its driver.

The next race, in Austria, gave the 917 its first victory for Siffert/Ahrens in a short-tail, but it was in the subsequent development on that circuit, aided by John Wyer's team, that the 1970 shape was evolved. By creating a wedge, raising the waist and extending the line into the tail, the stability was considerably improved at the expense of a drag factor increase to 0·46, but this brought a circuit lap improvement of 3½ per cent due to the body shape alone.

The factory ran the racing effort of 1969 but for 1970 this was split between John Wyer's Gulf organisation and Porsche Salzburg. The car I tested, 917-013, was one of the original batch of 25 but

wasn't used during 1969, joining the Wyer team— the team had seven cars to play with so the cars weren't used too hard—to be driven mostly by Pedro Rodriguez.

Its first outing was at Sebring where it was driven into fourth place by the Rodriguez/Kinnunen pairing. Sebring was the only race that the 917s didn't win when they competed—908s won the Targa Florio and the Nürburgring; new hub bearings failed on all the 917s and Ferrari, who had belatedly joined the fray with his 512S, won his only race.

For 1970 the cars were running with four-speed gearboxes except at Le Mans where the speed band was greater. This car went on to win the Monza 1000 Km with the 4·5-litre engine, while others were using 4·9-litres. The extra capacity came from a stroke increase to 70·4 mm to give 600 bhp and 415 lb-ft at 6400 rpm.

At this point the car seems to have been lent to the makers of the film *Le Mans* for there it ended the first stage of its career resulting in the need for a new chassis. Obviously the serious business of Porsche racing continued and the 917s continued their winning ways with little further development. Le Mans, of course, posed its own problems; modified nose and after-deck shapes and wings on fixed fins kept the drag factor down to 0·36 with reasonable stability, although John Wyer ran three of the current short-tail cars with a small wing across the rear gulley—as the car now has. All three Wyer cars retired with two engine failures and an accident, while the race went to the 4·5-litre short-tail of

Attwood/Hans Herrman entered by Porsche Salzburg from the 4·5-litre long-tail entered privately by the Martini Racing Team. The Elford/Ahrens Salzburg car broke a valve after 18 hours.

For 1971 917-013 came back into the fold with its reinforced roll cage and heavier fire-extinguishing system countered by a new body construction using an epoxy-glass-fibre laminate for greater strength and lightness. Ferrari hadn't had much of a look-in during 1970 but had produced the 512M for 1971 with more power and less weight, which prompted Porsche to seek a little more power bringing the capacity up to 4998 cc with the bore up to 86·8 cc; Nikasil liners, a nickel-silicum layer on the aluminium cylinders, proved to have less friction, so the extra 90 cc appeared to increase the output to 630 bhp at 8300 rpm from 600 bhp, although the torque increase was understandably less dramatic at lower revs.

For its first 1971 outing 013 was driven at Daytona by Pedro Rodriguez/Jackie Oliver; the K-tails had been further modified to have a lower tail with tabs at the back and stabilising fins—downthrust was reduced but the drag factor was improved to 0·39. However, the Wyer team mostly preferred to keep what were substantially their 1970 Le Mans tails. A 4·9-litre engine giving 580 bhp was used in 013 with two alternators fitted and was geared to pull 209 mph at 8450 rpm; although Donohue was faster during practice in the Sunoco 512M, Rodriguez/Oliver won. The pair were fourth at Sebring in another 917 to the winning Elford/Larousse car run this year by the Martini Racing Team who had replaced Porsche Salzburg.

The car wasn't at the BOAC 1000 Km but it won at the Monza 1000 Km where the 4·99-litre engine

was being used. Here the car used the standard K-tail with its vertical fins for the higher speeds; again it was geared to pull 208 mph but at 8600 rpm. Although third gear failed seven laps from the end, they still won at 146·5 mph from Siffert/Bell. At both Daytona and Monza the car averaged 5·9 mpg!

At Spa it was again a Wyer 1, 2 with 014 and 015 with Rodriguez/Oliver winning at 154·7 mph while Siffert left the lap record at 162 mph. For Le Mans Porsche provided the new long tail cars; these had been designed with the fashionable low squared front preventing too much air going underneath, while the rear body incorporated wheel spats around ever wider wheels. Oliver was timed at 240 mph during the April test week-end. However, all three long-tail cars retired, although Rodriguez/Oliver led for much of the time until an oil pipe broke. A pair of short-tails came first and second for the Martini/Wyer teams. Next outing for 013 was the Austrian race for which the engine was back to 4·99-litres, and the five-speed box, while the body was the JW K-tail; with Attwood partnering Rodriguez the car won again, despite a battery change which dropped them back to seventh. Two JW cars went to Watkins Glen and came second and third to the 3-litre Alfa Romeo; these had taken the Targa Florio and Brands Hatch from the Porsches. However, 013 went down to two non-championship 1000 Km races at the end of the season, Barcelona and Montlhéry; wet racing let a Chevron beat Bell/Van Lennep round the twisty Montuich Park, but 013 won its last works outing in the rain at Montlhéry, completing its second 1000 Km race with only a stop for a plug change in between.

The Martini Porsche 917K which Marko and van Lennep drove to victory at Le Mans in 1971

Small British kit cars

As in the world of Grand Prix racing, the Ford Motor Company and Hewland Engineering have launched many an enthusiast into racing car production; before them it was Climax engines and BMC gearboxes, or Bristols or Jaguars. By contrast the production of a chassis and body was relatively simple; without Ford and Hewland there would have been many fewer formulae competing on our national tracks. This combination started back in 1960 when independent tuners seized upon the Anglia engine for Formula Junior, and Mike Hewland started modifying Renault and Volkswagen gearboxes, and that made it easier for Lotus and many other constructors to build mid-engined cars.

It wasn't long before the relationship between Ford and Lotus moved a bit closer with the debut of the Ford-Lotus Twin-Cam at the Nürburgring in 1962. It was installed in a Lotus 23 which had been shown at the Racing Car show in that January powered by a Cosworth-tuned 1100 cc Ford. At the end of May, Jim Clark led the Nürburgring 1000 Km for 11 laps against the might of Ferrari and Porsche; admittedly it was a damp and drying track and the greater power of the rivals meant that they gradually ate into the lead, but it was the Lotus that removed itself from competition as Clark suffered from too much braking on the rear and eventually spun off when the box jumped out of gear. It was an impressive debut for an engine described by its designer in *Autocar* as 'fitted with a twin ohc conversion of the Ford Classic engine, enlarged to 1500 cc'. In production terms the engine went on to power all the Lotus Elan/Europa range, and two versions of the Lotus-Cortina.

It was also the engine in the Lotus 23B (coupled to a Hewland gearbox) in the early one I tried, so early that it had started life as an 1100, but had been uprated along the way. The 23 was a space-frame car with by then conventional racing suspension—twin wishbones at the front, and at the rear single upper link and inverted lower wishbone plus trailing arms; a certain amount of adjustability was built into the suspension, but in 1963 we were still in an area of relatively narrow tyres so there wasn't a lot to be gained by increased sophistication, then—the car was on more modern tyres when I tried it.

A Lotus 23 is very much a product of the post-1950s. You get down into it, treading carefully as you lower yourself in; doors and bonnet are held down by springs. Once in and strapped down it is quite a comfortable position, semi-reclining with your feet level with the front hubs but without much elbow room; a small steering wheel is at arms' length.

On the right is a small lever for the change to the Hewland five-speed box, unlike the original 1100's central change by whippy wand. I gathered that the engine had a steel-capped bottom end which was good for 9000 rpm, but that the rest of it was a little more limited and produced around 160 bhp. The owner used 7800 rpm so I kept to 7000 rpm, which leaves some in hand if an unfamiliar change is muffed. Despite an impressive power/weight ratio which should be more than that of a Lister-Jaguar, it didn't feel as fast once into the third gear band—the difference between a torquey 3·8-litre 'six' and a rather flatter 1·6-litre 'four'. The Hewland wasn't ideal with rather a gap across the gate from 2/3 to 4/5 but I never actually missed it.

At speed down the straight one is conscious of being in a light car, as you can see the bonnet flutter as speed rises and the rear bodywork seemed to be fluttering too, but it is when you tread on the brakes and pull up far too soon for the corner that you realise how light—quoted weight for the 1100 was 900 lb! Having got used to that after accelerating again it became a question of going ever deeper into the corner to a point almost unbelievable against that for heavier cars. Under braking there was slight weaving and the tail always felt as if it wanted to wag on the way into the corners but it never did; even a deliberate lift-off in mid-Becketts required little more than a mild adjustment of steering angle rather than correction. Under power, when there is enough surplus, the tail can be made to move out controllably. There is no roll apparent and there wasn't a great deal of feel through rather dead steering so you have to play it by seat of pants; but the 4·50M- and 5·25M-13-in tyres on 5- and 6-in wheels certainly grip well and point the car accurately. Visibility forwards is very good over the fall-away bonnet and you can take in most of what is happening behind you in a quick glance either side across the flat rear deck—there are mirrors, but...

Frank Nichols was another one to be involved in popular small sports-car racing with the Elva; his contender in this category was the Mk. VIIS powered at times by Ford or Porsche engines, but by BMW on this occasion. The appeal of the BMW 'four' stemmed from its relatively simple single ohc hemi-valve layout and the fact that it was possible to bore the standard 1800Ti unit out to 2-litres, and generate some 184 bhp at 7200 rpm. It still started

Above: Jim Clark gave the Lotus 23 a sensational debut at the Nürburgring in 1962
Below: the Lotus 23 with later Hewland transmission

with a Hewland gearbox although this one too had been replaced by a later, heavier unit for reliability. The BMW 'four' is never very smooth at tickover in racing tune, so it pays to get under way as soon as possible. Acceleration isn't neck-snapping, just continuous with a very useful power/weight ratio. With a suspension layout that is basically exactly the same as that of the Lotus it isn't surprising that they felt much the same — tyre sizes were the same too but the Elva had wheels an inch wider. The steering was better, though, in that you could feel the front end working, slipping outwards, and this could be balanced by power to a neutral attitude or a slide on tighter corners.

Although neither of these cars were designed to take the Dunlop M-section tyres, which give a wider contact patch, both had been adapted to them by stiffening springs to reduce suspension travel.

The BMW unit was still a good alternative in 1966 when the first of Derek Bennett's Chevron B8s appeared from Bolton. He had built up a good reputation with clubman's cars and moved into the International field with the B8, achieving homologation for it as a 50-off sports car during 1967. The B8s were a great success with the privateers who liked to enjoy their long-distance racing; it was strong with a space-frame chassis reinforced by steel and aluminium sheeting, to become almost a monocoque chassis, with bolt on glassfibre bodywork; it was well sorted and the BMW engine seemed quite happy to keep going for 1000 km at a time. In principle the suspension design was the same as for the Lotus 23, but by now we were using newer tyres of lower profile and by the time I tried one in 1970, the rim widths were 9 and 12-in, the same as for the later Chevron B16.

I was warned that the engine would sound like a bag of old nails when I started it up, and it did. It felt as though all the solid engine mounts were loose; everything rattled and shook at idling speed. But with 2000 rpm showing it all smoothed down and my confidence returned.

It was some time since I had driven a mid-engined GT on a circuit, so I went carefully, deliberately overbraking and feeling my way round the gate pattern of the Hewland five-speed box. It was a rather imprecise movement, but a throw of the lever to the right corner found the right ratio and revs didn't have to be too precise with the dog clutch engagement.

Sitting in the car I was rather conscious of being hemmed in by the beetle-browed screen top, with anti-sun green strip, and the rear bulkhead being a single wall of aluminium with a rear view slot; the forward view was good because of the thin pillars. The only instrumentation was a rev counter and combined oil pressure/water temperature gauge with a few warning lights — and a disconnected speedometer. The pedals were nicely spaced and a fourth pedal gave a good clutch footrest. The leather-rimmed wheel was placed just right for me and the steering was quite light, getting heavier with more lock and cornering power.

In the first tentative forays I didn't use anywhere near the 7000 permitted rpm and thus appreciated the tractability of the BMW unit tuned to give around 186 bhp at 7200 rpm; it pulled with the usual rattly Weber chug from around 3500 rpm quite happily. With this output and about 1230 lb, acceleration was quite impressive. With Silverstone gearing it pulled about 127 mph on the downhill Hanger Straight.

The B8 feels very surefooted and has a useful amount of weight up front to give a well-balanced feel. There was some kickback through the steering but it was nicely weighted with the right gearing. Through Copse (a bit greasy that day) and Becketts the car would just begin to oversteer, which never required more than just a premature unwinding of applied lock. At the adversely cambered Club Corner, the car understeered a little, provoking some squeal from the front tyres, but this all felt quite undramatic and you knew what was happening. Accelerating flat through Abbey the front developed a slight rolling lurch on the bumps, but generally I wasn't conscious of the circuit being anything but dead smooth so well did the suspension work.

Meanwhile Lotus had inserted the Twin-Cam Ford into the Lotus 47 Europa, which was homologated as an Appendix J group 4 sports car with completely revised Rose-jointed racing suspension to take 9 and 10½-in rim wheels with tyres that would have suited a Formula 1 car at the beginning of that year, 1968. This was one of the works cars in Gold Leaf Team Lotus colours with all the available extras; the engine used a Cosworth dry sump bottom end, BRM reworked head and cams and T-J fuel injection to give around 172 rpm at 7500 rpm; the gearbox on this nominal descendant of a road car was the ubiquitous Hewland FT200.

It should have felt just like a Chevron B8 but it didn't; however hard you work on a road car it just isn't possible to make it into a track car and stay within the rules. In performance they felt pretty similar but the Lotus began to feel rather light at the top end of its speed range; its steering was a little dead but still transmitted enough to tell you of changing adhesion. It was the slightly lurchy front end that put me off, a mixture of roll and pitch — doubtless firmer damping would have helped, but perhaps the chassis just wasn't stiff enough to take the grip that was being fed into it.

By 1969 Cosworth were well into production of the DFV (double four valve) Grand Prix unit and had produced a four cylinder equivalent, the FVA based on the Ford 1500 block; this was capable of turning out some 240 bhp at 9500 rpm in Formula 2 form, but the one that appealed to most of the sports car builders was the 1790 cc FVC with a longer stroke than the FVA in the 1600 cross-flow block — with 245 bhp at 8500 rpm and more torque it was a much more useable unit.

I first met this in a Chevron B16, the logical development of the B8 in both aerodynamics and suspension design. By mid-1970 the coupe B16 had been homologated as a group 5 car — 25-off — but most of the races were for mixed group 5/6 in a

special 2-litre championship, and many B16s were cut down to open B16S/B19. However driving the B16 was quite an experience in modern design, highlighting the changes that had taken place over the years of rapid development.

New screen regulations had allowed 4 in off the B8 height so the car was a lot sleeker; it was a bit like sitting in a greenhouse as the side windows go almost to the centre of the roof and visibility was excellent. It was like being in an open car without any buffeting.

Going down the pit road it was obvious that the B16 was a much faster car than the B8 and that everything was tauter. You needed to keep the engine blipping when at rest and there wasn't a lot of useful power much below 6000 rpm, but from there to 8500–9000 rpm it really took off with a hard urgent buzz; it was remarkably smooth and it didn't seem to get much noisier, so you needed to watch the rev counter.

The suspension seemed well nigh perfect with only the occasional jerk from a bad bump which didn't upset the line. There was instant response to the wheel and you could feel exactly what was happening; it was set up to understeer slightly, but able to tighten its exit line on sharper corners. The

The Elva Mk. 7S was Frank Nichols' answer to the Lotus 23, with BMW power (*top*). The same unit was also used in the Chevron B8 (*above*)

Above: a Lotus 47 in racing trim
Below: favourite 2-litre car, John Burton's Chevron B16, which gave the author a 106 mph lap at Silverstone—before the Woodcote chicane was constructed

B16's competitors were mostly open cars in the European 2-litre Championship but Chevron still managed to win it in 1970; it was Lola's turn in 1971 with the T210. I tried Chevron's contender, the B19, and the 1970 Lola T210 a year after driving the B16, but by now we were into an area of total adjustability, so that performance is very much a function of the driver's sorting ability and the engine maintaining its power—both were using FVC units. I remember the Chevron as having an almost go-kart response with superb behaviour, but the Lola had been set up differently and was too soft for my taste. Both Chevron and Lola were beaten in 1972 by the Osella Abarths, so it wasn't just a Ford championship.

However Ford and Hewland still continue to provide the motive power pack for so many cars from Formula Ford to Formula 1, but between them they were responsible for the kit-car revolution that made racing so available and so close, but the cars so indistinguishable. The classic era ended in the late 1960s.

Index